SUMMARY OF CONTENTS

FLEMING'S
FUNDAMENTALS OF LAW

ESSAY EXAMINATION WRITING WORKBOOK
Volume 2

by

Jeff Alan Fleming
Attorney at Law

Susan Patricia Sneidmiller
Attorney at Law

LEARN TO WRITE . . . THE RIGHT WAY®

Published by: Fleming's Fundamentals of Law
26170 Enterprise Way, Suite 500, Lake Forest, CA 92630
(949) 770-7030 ◆ (800) LAW EXAM
FAX (949) 454-8556 ◆ WEB www.ffol.com
E-MAIL info@ffol.com

Distributed by: Legal Books Distributing
2740 E Regal Park Dr.
Anaheim, CA 92806
(800) 200-7110

MANAGING WRITER AND EDITOR

Susan Patricia Sneidmiller
Attorney at Law

SUPERVISING WRITER AND EDITOR

Jeff Alan Fleming
Attorney at Law

CONTRIBUTING WRITERS

Professor Glenn Koppel
Western State University College of Law

Professor Todd Brower
Western State University College of Law

LAYOUT

Donald Bayley II
IMAGEN Company, Irvine, CA.

FLEMING'S FUNDAMENTALS OF LAW
ESSAY EXAMINATION WRITING WORKBOOK

LEGAL MAXIM

**"Out of the Facts, the Issue Arises
Without Facts, There is no Issue"**

I. GENERAL CONSIDERATIONS

The basic fundamentals of legal writing can be summarized in a simple statement: Legal writing is the process of applying the individual elements from the specific rules of law to specific factual situations upon which justifiable and well organized conclusions are based.

The ability to communicate clearly and concisely in the above manner must be learned and perfected. The earlier you learn the process, the more manageable your study of the law will become. The foundation upon which the technique of legal writing is built involves three distinct skills that are learned individually and then integrated with practice. The purpose of this book is to identify and demonstrate the skills that you must master as the prerequisite to producing an effective passing essay examination.

II. SKILLS TESTED

A. Analysis

Most law school examinations are presented in the form of factual situations referred to as hypotheticals. The Essay Examination Writing Workbook deals solely with this form of testing.

Analysis is the ability to recognize the facts from the hypothetical that raise the legal issues and to then apply the elements from the applicable rule of law to those issues.

You must be able to read and comprehend the facts as they are given. You will soon realize that it is the facts given in the hypothetical that raise the legal issues. Because of this, you must never underestimate the importance of reading and comprehending the facts. "Fact Sensitivity" is the basis of sound legal reasoning.

The recommended steps that you should follow in sequence for proper legal analysis are:

1. Review the call of the question located at the end of the hypothetical before reading the hypothetical facts. This will help orient your thinking process to the area of law being tested. The call will often narrow the issues and parties that you are to address.

2. Read the hypothetical at least twice from a factual perspective to understand and comprehend the facts.

3. Read the hypothetical for a third time from a legal perspective at which point you may begin analyzing and issue spotting. Remember, the issue arises from the facts.

There are numerous methods that you may utilize to improve your issue spotting. You should seriously consider the following suggestions that will assist you in this area.

1. Develop approaches and issue checklists for each subject. Use the table of contents in your casebook, your class syllabus and/or the table of contents in a commercial outline as your source for development of this tool.

2. Analyze every hypothetical paying special attention to adjectives and adverbs, which are descriptive words, and verbs, which are action words. These types of facts are generally issues. Dates and times should never be ignored for the same reason.

3. Analyze each sentence of each paragraph in every hypothetical. Rarely, if ever, does a hypothetical contain totally irrelevant facts. With practice, you will learn to distinguish background facts from issue facts.

4. Analyze every issue by role playing each party's position. This will help you identify counter-arguments to the issues that demand extended analysis.

5. Review and write multiple examinations for each subject area in which you will be tested before sitting for your examination.

Begin the analysis of every hypothetical by allocating approximately 5-7 minutes to the steps suggested in this section.

B. Organization

It is essential for you to be able to organize your issues and arguments in a logical sequence. Students who see every issue, but are unorganized when presenting the discussion of these issues, will not pass the examination.

The call of the question will often specify the order in which the issues/parties are to be organized. If so, never deviate from the call unless absolutely necessary.

When the call of the question is very general and does not specify the order in which the issues are to be presented, (i.e., Discuss) you may organize according to:

1. The issues that each party will assert,
2. The chronology of events,
3. The sequence that is most logical based on the hypothetical. The approaches that you have developed for each subject will help you to determine the organizational sequence.

Effective outlining for 10-15 minutes will greatly assist you when organizing your issues. To conserve time, remember to abbreviate words/phrases as much as possible in your outline. You should strive to learn proper outlining as demonstrated by the model outlines that accompany each of the hypotheticals presented in this book. At first, you may become frustrated with the technique because it is new to you. Do not let your frustration get in the way of your learning process. With practice, the outlining technique will become simple and reflexive.

Do not be fooled into thinking that the time spent outlining will detract from the time necessary to complete the final written answer. When done properly, outlining will afford you the opportunity to think through and strategize your analysis and organization before you commit yourself in the blue book.

Outlining each issue as demonstrated will enable you to separate major issues from minor issues, eliminate non-issues, adjust your organization when necessary, and determine how much time you must allocate to the writing of each issue. In essence, proper outlining will focus your analysis. This will ultimately save you time. For example, if you see on your outline that you have an issue that has multiple elements and facts, you will know that you will have to allocate more time to that issue than you will to another issue with fewer elements and facts.

Unless otherwise indicated, law school examinations must be completed within 60 minutes. You should strive to spend the first 10-20 minutes analyzing, organizing, and outlining before you begin writing in your blue book.

C. Writing

You must be able to demonstrate your ability to apply the elements of the applicable rule of law to facts in the hypothetical with a blend of precision and simplicity. The most efficient and effective method to accomplish this goal is through the use of the IRAC system. This method is thoroughly demonstrated in each model answer provided in this book.

To use the IRAC system, you should clearly indicate what the issue is in the form of a headnote. Follow the issue with the specific rule of law that applies. Then argue all applicable facts in relation to each and every element of the stated rule. If an element has a recognized "buzz word" associated with it, bring that "buzz word" into the discussion when addressing the facts that relate to that element.

When the analysis is completed, you must give a final conclusion. Because minimal point value is allocated to the conclusion, it should be no more than a one or two sentence summary of the stated issue.

EXAMPLE OF IRAC CIVIL PROCEDURE ISSUE

(I) **Res Judicata**

(R) (1) A valid final judgment on the merits precludes a reassertion of the (2) same cause of action in a subsequent action between the (3) same parties or their privies.

(A) Worker's suit against Hospital was a (1) valid final judgment on the merits as to the Doctor's independent contractor status and lack of negligence.

Doctor will contend that the first suit, Worker v. Hospital, was a negligence action and the second suit brought by Paula was for damages she sustained as a result of Worker's wrongful death. Since a wrongful death action sounds in negligence, the causes of action were the (2) same. Paula's suit in State C is precluded because it is a reassertion of the same cause of action in the subsequent action.

However, Doctor was not a (3) party to the first suit. Since he was found not to have been the agent of the Hospital due to his status as an independent contractor, he was not a privy to the action.

(C) The doctrine of res judicata is not applicable.

The final written product should be completed within the remaining 40-50 minutes of the examination period. If you have analyzed and organized thoroughly, you should have no problem finishing the examination within the suggested time frame.

Strive for a blue book that averages between 6-9 pages in length. Remember, it is the quality, not the quantity, of the written word that will establish success.

III. RECOMMENDED USE OF THE ESSAY EXAMINATION WRITING WORKBOOK

The Essay Examination Writing Workbook is divided into the three substantive subject areas of Civil Procedure, Real Property and Evidence. Each of these subjects is presented through five hypotheticals with corresponding model outlines and model answers. Each hypothetical emphasizes a different area of the substantive law in the designated subject. Combined, the selected hypotheticals cover the entire subject and will expose the student to the issues and arguments most likely to be tested in Civil Procedure, Real Property and Evidence during the first or second year of law school and on the State Bar Examination.

When proceeding through the materials presented in the Essay Examination Writing Workbook, you will derive the optimum benefit by following these recommended steps:

1. Read the first hypothetical presented in the section designated "Civil Procedure". For the reasons discussed previously, be sure to fully understand the call of the question and the facts.

2. When you fully understand the facts, begin issue spotting. Use the IRAC outline worksheet provided. List the issues in the (I) column, the elements of each issue in the (R) column, the corresponding facts that prove or disprove each element in the (A) column, and the conclusion in the (C) column. With practice, this technique will become automatic. Review your outline. Add any further relevant data. Delete irrelevant data. Make organizational adjustments if necessary.

3. Upon completion of your outline, turn to the model outline provided. Compare your work. Identify the issues, elements and/or key facts that you have missed. Add those to your own outline. Compare your organization. Rethink your analysis if you find errors with your organization. Adjust your outline accordingly.

   You should constantly strive to produce outlines that are similar to the model outlines in this book. Abbreviate words and phrases on your outline wherever possible to conserve time. With practice, you will develop a form of shorthand that will make your outlining time more efficient.

4. Write your final answer in a blue book using your outline as your guide. Write every issue in the IRAC format. Pay special attention to your analysis, always discussing the facts in relation to the individual elements of the rule. In this way, you will "use the facts rather than merely repeating them."

5. Compare your written answer to the model answer provided. Identify inconsistencies in your IRAC. Review your analysis carefully in comparison to the model answer looking for weaknesses in factual discussion or missed analysis. Rewrite the analysis if you have missed major facts or arguments. Then proceed to the next hypothetical and repeat the process.

The first few hypotheticals should be analyzed, organized and written at your own pace without concern for the amount of time spent on the question. It will take practice to become familiar with the IRAC form of outlining and writing. Do not rush yourself.

As you proceed to the fifth or sixth hypothetical, you will become more proficient with the suggested techniques. At that point, you should begin to adhere to the time constraints imposed under examination conditions. You will then have an appreciation for the manner in which you must pace yourself to complete the exercise within the designated time period.

Do not expect to immediately articulate every argument as clearly as that demonstrated in the model answer. The ease upon which your legal writing skills develop will depend upon how much time you devote to practicing those skills. The more hypotheticals that you write, the more proficient your writing will become.

Practice is the essential ingredient that will help you develop the skills and confidence necessary to build the foundation for sound legal writing.

IV. PREPARING FOR LAW SCHOOL EXAMINATIONS

The key to performing well on law school examinations is preparation. Preparation involves a two prong process. First, you must learn the rules of law. Second, you must demonstrate how to apply those rules in the context of a factual hypothetical. Too many students make the mistake of placing all their emphasis on the first prong at the expense of the equally important second prong. The student who allows himself to fall into this trap usually produces essays that are too law oriented, conclusary, and weak in factual analysis. The Essay Examination Writing Workbook will help you overcome these pitfalls.

Be sure to approach each hypothetical in this book as indicated. In this way, you will maximize the development of the skills that you must demonstrate for success in law school and on the Bar Examination.

GOOD LUCK!!

SECTION V

CIVIL PROCEDURE

CIVIL PROCEDURE

LEARN TO WRITE . . . THE RIGHT WAY®

CIVIL PROCEDURE QUESTION #1

ARNOLD/BATES v. MANCO/STORCO

Arnold and Bates, residents of State Z, are plaintiffs in an action brought in the United States District Court in State X against Manco, a State Y corporation, and Storco, a State X corporation.

Manco's office and plant are located in State Y. At no time has Manco had an office or salesmen in State X. Storco's sole place of business is in State X.

The complaint alleges that each of the plaintiffs sustained serious personal injuries when a blade broke in an electric lawn mower while the mower was being demonstrated by a clerk in Storco's store in State X. Each plaintiff asked for damages in the sum of $80,000.

The mower had been manufactured by Manco and shipped to Roe Distributors in State Z. Roe had a contract with Manco to act as exclusive distributor of Manco products in eleven states including states X and Z.

Process was served personally on the president of Manco at Manco's office in State Y and on the president of Storco at its office in State X.

Thereafter the following occurred:

(1) Manco moved to dismiss on the ground that the court had no jurisdiction over it. The motion to dismiss was denied.

(2) Both defendants filed motions asserting misjoinder of parties plaintiff and defendant. The trial court ruled there was no misjoinder and denied the motions.

(3) Storco filed a counterclaim against Arnold for $900 alleged to be due for merchandise previously sold to Arnold. Arnold's motion to strike the counterclaim was granted.

(4) Manco filed a cross-claim against Storco for $12,000 alleged to be due for merchandise previously sold by Manco to Storco. Storco's motion to strike the cross-claim was denied.

Assuming that all appropriate grounds were argued in support of and in opposition to each of the above motions, was the trial court correct in each of its rulings? Discuss.

IRAC OUTLINE SHEET

(I)	(R)	(A)	(C)

Model Outlines Serve As A Demonstration Only. Students Should Abbreviate Words & Phrases Whenever Possible To Keep Outline Time Between 15 - 20 Minutes.

EXAMPLE OF PROPER IRAC OUTLINE

ARNOLD & BATES (A/B) v. MANCO/STORECO (M/S)

(1) DISMISSAL FOR LACK OF JURISDICTION

(I)	(R)	(A)	(C)
SUBJECT MATTER JURISDICTION	Power Of Court To Hear If:	Action brought in U.S. District Court State X Complaint alleges A/B sustained serious personal injuries when lawn mower blade broke during a demonstration	Subject Matter Jurisdiction Present Court Properly Ruled
	Complete Diversity	A/B resident of State Z M a State Y corporation/office & plant located in Y S a State X corporation/sole place of business in State X	
	Amount In Controversy	A/B each asked for damages in sum of $80,000	
PERSONAL JURISDICTION	Power To Bind Person In Controversy Minimum Contacts	M State Y corporation sued in State X M at no time had offices or salesmen in State X	Minimum Contacts
	Purposeful Availment	Mower manufactured by M/shipped to Roe Distributors in State Z	
	Fair Play/Substantial Justice	Roe had contract with M to act as exclusive distributor of M products in 11 states including X & Z	
SERVICE OF PROCESS	Procedural Due Process Notice/Opportunity To Be Heard	Process served Personally on president of M at M's office in State Y	Proper Service Personal Jurisdiction Court Properly Ruled

(2) MOTION FOR MISJOINDER

(I)	(R)	(A)	(C)
PERMISSIVE JOINDER OF PLAINTIFFS	Right to Relief Asserted Jointly	A/B brought an action against M/S Each plaintiff asked for damages in sum of $80,000	
	Right Arises Out Of Same Transaction	Each plaintiff sustained serious personal injuries when blade broke during mower demonstration	Proper Joinder of Plaintiffs Court Properly Ruled
	Common Question Law/Fact	Liability of M/S	
PERMISSIVE JOINDER OF DEFENDANTS	Right to Relief Asserted Jointly	M/S co-defendants	
	Right Arises Out Of Same Transaction	Mower demonstration	Proper Joinder Court Properly Ruled
	Common Question Law/Fact	Causation/liability	

(3) S's COUNTERCLAIM AGAINST A

(I)	(R)	(A)	(C)
COMPULSORY COUNTERCLAIM	Claim Arises Out Of Same Transaction of Complaint	Complaint alleged personal injuries from lawn mower accident $900 counterclaim for merchandise previously sold	No Compulsory Counterclaim
	No Independent Subject Matter Required	Ø	
SUPPLEMENTAL JURISDICTION	No Independent Subject Matter Jurisdiction	S a State X corporation A, a resident of Z $900 claim	No Supplemental Jurisdiction Court Properly Ruled
	Sufficient Relation To Main Claim	Each plaintiff sustained serious personal injuries when blade broke during mower demonstration S filed counterclaim against A for $900 supra	

(4) MANCO'S CROSS-CLAIM AGAINST S

(I)	(R)	(A)	(C)
CROSS-CLAIM	Claim Relates To Transaction	$12,000 for merchandise previously sold to S	Invalid Cross-Claim
	Subject Of Complaint	Complaint alleged personal injuries from lawn mower accident	
SUPPLEMENTAL JURISDICTION	No Independent Subject Matter Jurisdiction	M a State Y corporation S a State X corporation $12,000 for merchandise	No Supplemental Jurisdiction Court Improperly Ruled
	Sufficient Relation To Main Claim	$12,000 for merchandise previously sold by M to S	

EXAMPLE OF IRAC CIVIL PROCEDURE ISSUE

(I) **Subject Matter Jurisdiction - Diversity**

(R) A federal court has the power to hear and determine a particular type of controversy if (1) complete diversity exists between the plaintiff and defendant, and (2) the amount in controversy exceeds $75,000 exclusive of interest and costs.

(A) Arnold and Bates brought suit in the U.S. District Court in State X. Their complaint alleged serious personal injuries sustained when a lawn mower blade broke during a demonstration. Both Arnold and Bates are citizens of State Z. Defendant Manco is a State Y corporation with its office and plant located in State Y. As such, Manco is considered a citizen of State Y where it is incorporated and has its principal place of business. Defendant Storco is a State X corporation with its sole place of business in State X. It would be considered a citizen of State X. Therefore, because no defendant is a citizen of the same state as any plaintiff, there is (1) complete diversity among the parties.

Arnold and Bates have each alleged damages of $80,000. Each of their claims satisfies the jurisdictional requirement for (2) an amount in controversy exceeding $75,000.00 exclusive of interest and costs. Therefore, the U.S. District Court has the power to hear the controversy.

(C) The U.S. District Court has diversity subject matter jurisdiction. Therefore, Manco's motion to dismiss was properly denied.

SUGGESTED MODEL ANSWER

ARNOLD AND BATES v. MANCO/STORCO

(1) DISMISSAL FOR LACK OF JURISDICTION

a. Subject Matter Jurisdiction - Diversity

A federal court has the power to hear and determine a particular type of controversy if complete diversity exists between the plaintiff and defendant, and the amount in controversy exceeds $75,000 exclusive of interest and costs.

Arnold and Bates brought suit in the U.S. District Court in State X. Their complaint alleged serious personal injuries sustained when a lawn mower blade broke during a demonstration. Both Arnold and Bates are citizens of State Z. Defendant Manco is a State Y corporation with its office and plant located in State Y. As such, Manco is considered a citizen of State Y where it is incorporated and has its principal place of business. Defendant Storco is a State X corporation with its sole place of business in State X. It would be considered a citizen of State X. Therefore, because no defendant is a citizen of the same state as any plaintiff, there is complete diversity among the parties.

Arnold and Bates have each alleged damages of $80,000. Each of their claims satisfies the jurisdictional requirement for an amount in controversy exceeding $75,000 exclusive of interest and costs. Therefore, the U.S. District Court has the power to hear the controversy.

The U.S. District Court has diversity subject matter jurisdiction. Therefore, Manco's motion to dismiss was properly denied.

b. Personal Jurisdiction - Due Process

Assuming the court is authorized under State X's long arm statute to assert personal jurisdiction over Manco, does the exercise of personal jurisdiction over Manco comport with the requirements of the due process clause?

Under the case of **International Shoe**, the court may exercise jurisdiction over a defendant who is not present in the forum state only if that defendant has minimum contacts with the forum state such that the maintenance of the suit does not offend traditional notions of fair play and substantial justice.

Manco was a State Y corporation. At no time was it physically present in State X nor did it have offices or salesmen in State X. Manco did not directly market its mowers in State X. However, it manufactured lawn mowers in State Y and shipped them to Roe Distributors in State Z. Manco had a contract with Roe making Roe Manco's exclusive distributor of Manco products in eleven states including State X. Manco indirectly transacted business in State X indirectly through Roe and made contracts enforceable in State X with Roe.

These ongoing activities give rise to obligations related to such business practice. Manco manifested its intent to serve the market in State X by its deliberate distribution of its lawn mowers in that state. In doing so, Manco purposefully availed itself of the economic benefits and protections of State X through its ongoing business contacts.

Manco purposefully set up this chain of distribution into State X. Manco directly benefited from the State X market. Therefore, Manco should reasonably expect to defend a products liability suit in State X arising out of its product distribution and sale there. To the extent that Arnold and Bates' claims arose out of Manco's lawn mower sales in State X, Manco must be subject to the burdens of litigation associated with doing business in that forum.

Manco's authorization of lawn mower distribution in State X carries with it foreseeable products liability consequences in that state. Manco's acts constitute sufficient minimum contacts with State X such that the maintenance of the suit in that jurisdiction does not offend traditional notions of fair play and substantial justice for purposes of litigation fairness.

The court properly denied Manco's motion.

c. Notice - Service of Process

The defendant must receive service of process allowing notice reasonably calculated to apprise it of the pendency of the action and an opportunity to be heard sufficient to satisfy the requirements of constitutional procedural due process (**Mullane.**)

The facts indicate that process was served personally on Manco's president at Manco's office in State Y. Since the president of a company is generally authorized to accept service of process on behalf of that company, service of process on Manco's president at the Manco office provides Manco with notice reasonably calculated to apprise it of the pendency of the Arnold/Bates action against it. This notice also affords Manco an opportunity to present any objection to the service of process that will be heard in the court in which the action was filed.

Therefore, service of process on Manco's president at Manco's office in state Y is sufficient to satisfy the requirements of constitutional procedural due process. State X may exercise personal jurisdiction over Manco.

The court properly denied Manco's motion.

(2) DEFENDANT'S MOTION ALLEGING MISJOINDER

a. Permissive Joinder of Plaintiffs

All persons may be joined as plaintiffs or defendants in one action when a right to relief is asserted by or against them jointly, severally or, in the alternative, the right to relief arises out of the same transaction or series of transactions and there is at least one question of law or fact common to all parties sought to be joined.

Arnold and Bates each alleged a right to relief in the amount of $80,000.00 in their complaint. As such, each has a joint interest in a damage recovery. Each plaintiff sustained serious personal injuries when a blade broke during a lawn mower demonstration. As such, their right to relief arose out of the same transaction.

Since liability of the respective defendants must be determined, a common question of law and fact exists.

Based on the theory of judicial economy, permissive joinder is allowed. The court properly denied the defendant's motion.

b. Permissive Joinder of Defendants

Defined supra.

Plaintiffs alleged that both defendants were liable for their injuries giving both plaintiffs the right to seek relief separately or jointly. They may, therefore, exercise their option to sue the defendants jointly.

Their claims arose out of the same transaction. Common questions of law and fact exist as previously shown.

Defendants were properly joined. The court properly denied defendant's motion.

(3) ARNOLD'S MOTION TO STRIKE STORCO'S COUNTERCLAIM AGAINST ARNOLD FOR $900.00

Compulsory Counterclaim

Where the defendant's claim against the plaintiff arises out of the same transaction as the claim set forth in the complaint, it is mandatory for the defendant to assert it by compulsory counterclaim or it will be barred. No independent subject matter jurisdiction is required.

Storco field a $900 counterclaim against Arnold for merchandise previously sold to him. Arnold's complaint alleged personal injuries resulting from an alleged lawn mower blade accident. Since Storco's claim did not arise out of the same transaction as the claim set forth in Arnold's complaint, it is not a proper compulsory counterclaim.

The court properly granted Arnold's motion to strike the compulsory counterclaim.

Supplemental Jurisdiction

Where a counterclaim does not have an independent basis of original federal subject matter jurisdiction, it can only be heard by the federal district court if the court can exercise supplemental jurisdiction. Under the Federal Supplemental Jurisdiction Statute, the court can exercise supplemental jurisdiction over the counterclaim if it is sufficiently related to the plaintiff's main claim so that the goal of judicial economy would be served. Under the federal common law of ancillary jurisdiction, which existed prior to the Supplemental Jurisdiction statute, courts could assert ancillary jurisdiction over compulsory counterclaims, but not permissive counterclaims.

There exists no coincidence of citizenship between Storco and Arnold as discussed under Call #1. However, Storco's $900 claim for merchandise previously sold does not meet the $75,000 amount in controversy requirement that is necessary for independent subject matter jurisdiction on the basis of diversity.

Therefore, because no independent basis for original federal subject matter jurisdiction exists concerning this counterclaim, it can only be heard by the federal district court if the court can exercise supplemental jurisdiction.

Arnold's complaint alleged personal injuries resulting from an alleged lawn mower blade accident during a demonstration by a Storco clerk at a Storco store. Storco filed a $900 counterclaim against Arnold for merchandise previously sold to him. Since Storco's counterclaim for merchandise previously sold to Arnold is completely unrelated to the main claim for personal injuries set forth in Arnold's complaint, under the Federal Supplemental Jurisdiction Statute, the federal court does not have the statutory authority to assert supplemental jurisdiction over Storco's counterclaim.

Applying the pre-statutory common law of ancillary jurisdiction, the court would have reached the same result by finding that Storco's counterclaim for failure to pay for merchandise previously sold to Arnold arises out of a different transaction or occurrence than Arnold's personal injury claim arising out of the defective lawn mower. Storco's counterclaim is permissive, not compulsory, and therefore requires its own independent basis of subject matter jurisdiction.

The court properly granted Arnold's motion to strike the compulsory counterclaim.

(4) STORCO'S MOTION TO STRIKE MANCO'S CROSS-CLAIM AGAINST STORCO FOR $12,000.00

Cross-Claim

In federal court actions, the defendant may set forth in the answer any claims which he has against a co-defendant that relate to the transaction or occurrence or to any property that is the subject of plaintiff's complaint.

Manco filed a $12,000 cross-claim against Storco, a co-defendant, for merchandise it had previously sold to Storco. Since the subject of the cross-claim was unrelated to the lawn mower accident that was the subject matter of Arnold and Bates' complaint, Manco's cross-claim was improper.

The court improperly denied Storco's motion to strike Manco's cross-claim.

Supplemental Jurisdiction

The Supplemental Jurisdiction Statute authorizes federal courts to assert supplemental jurisdiction over cross-claims that are not supported by an independent basis of subject matter jurisdiction if they are sufficiently related to claims that are supported by an independent basis of subject matter jurisdiction so that the goal of judicial economy will be achieved by hearing both claims in one federal court suit.

Manco filed a cross-claim against Storco for merchandise previously sold. Although Manco is from State Y and Storco is from State X, demonstrating a complete lack of coincidence of citizenship between them, Manco's $12,000 cross-claim against Storco for merchandise it had previously sold to Storco does not meet the $80,000 amount in controversy requirement.

As discussed, the subject of the cross-claim for the merchandise arises out of a completely different transaction. Thus, the cross-claim is completely unrelated to the main claim in the Arnold/Bates complaint.

Therefore, the court is not authorized to assert supplemental jurisdiction over the cross-claim.

The court would have reached the same result by applying the pre-statutory common law of ancillary jurisdiction. Under the law of ancillary jurisdiction, federal courts can assert ancillary jurisdiction over proper cross-claims. A proper cross-claim is one that arises out of the same transaction or occurrence as the main claim. As previously discussed, since Manco's cross-claim against Storco does not arise out of the same transaction or occurrence as the plaintiffs' claims against the defendants, the court could not assert ancillary jurisdiction over the cross-claim.

Thus, the court improperly denied Storco's motion to strike Manco's cross-claim.

CIVIL PROCEDURE #2

BYER v. SELER

Seler, a citizen of State S, and Byer, a citizen of State B, met in State B and signed a written contract by which Seler agreed to sell Whiteacre, located in State W, to Byer. The contract as written provided that the purchase price of Whiteacre was $80,000. Seler returned to State S and sent Byer a deed conveying good title to Whiteacre.

Byer did not send Seler any money, but brought an action against Seler for reformation of the contract to correct an alleged error in the contract price. Byer alleged that the agreed price was $60,000 and that the $80,000 figure in the contract was a typographical error. The action was brought in a federal district court in State B. Subject matter jurisdiction was based on diversity. Personal jurisdiction over Seler was based on service of process under State B's long-arm statute.

1. Seler moved to dismiss the action, alleging lack of both personal and subject matter jurisdiction. The motion was denied.

2. Seler then filed an answer asserting that the written contract accurately stated the agreed price. In addition, he counterclaimed for the $80,000 purchase price set forth in the contract and demanded a jury trial. Byer answered the counterclaim and moved to strike the demand for the jury trial. The motion was denied.

3. Seler then served Byer with interrogatories demanding responses to the following questions: "(a) Have you had Whiteacre appraised? (b) If so, state by whom, state the appraised value or values, and attach copies of all written reports received from all appraisers." Over Byer's timely objections to the interrogatories, the court ordered disclosure only of the identity of the appraisers and their appraised values.

4. At trial, Byer testified that the agreed price was $60,000 and that the $80,000 figure in the written contract was a typographical error. An appraiser testified on behalf of Byer that the value of Whiteacre when the contract was signed was, at most, $63,200. Byer rested his case. Seler testified that the agreed price was $80,000. The jury returned a verdict for Seler for $80,000, and judgment was entered accordingly. Byer promptly moved for a renewed motion for a judgment as a matter of law, or in the alternative, a new trial. The court granted the motion for a renewed motion for a judgment as a matter of law. No other motions were made during or after the trial.

   1. Did the court rule correctly on the motion to dismiss?
   2. Did the court rule correctly on the motion to strike the demand for the jury trial? Discuss.
   3. Did the court rule correctly on the objection to the interrogatories? Discuss.
   4. Was the evidence admitted at trial such that the court was correct in granting the renewed motion for a judgment as a matter of law? Discuss.
   5. What procedural argument or arguments should Seler have made in opposition to the renewed motion for a judgment as a matter of law? Discuss.

IRAC OUTLINE SHEET

(I)	(R)	(A)	(C)

EXAMPLE OF PROPER IRAC OUTLINE

BYER (B) v. SELER (S)

(1) COURT'S RULING ON MOTION TO DISMISS

(I)	(R)	(A)	(C)
(a) PERSONAL JURISDICTION Long Arm Statute	Power To Bind Defendant Personally Legislative Act Non-Resident Defendant	Personal jurisdiction over S was based on service of process under State B long arm statute State B's long arm statute S citizen of State S	Valid Long Arm
DOES TRANSACTION FALL WITHIN STATUTE	Tortious Act Must Occur In Forum Conservative - Where Harm Occurred Liberal - Wherever Harm Occurred	S & B met in State B/signed written contract by which S agreed to sell Whiteacre located in State W to B Contract contained an alleged typographical error in price	Transaction Within Liberal/Conservative
DUE PROCESS-MINIMUM CONTACTS	Minimum Contacts Purposeful Availment Fair Play/Substantial Justice	S, citizen of State S S & B met in State B/signed written contract supra S returned to State S/sent B deed conveying good title to Whiteacre supra	Minimum Contacts
SERVICE OF PROCESS	Procedural Due Process Notice/Opportunity To Be Heard	Personal Jurisdiction over S based on service of process under State B's long-arm statute	Proper Service Personal Jurisdiction Present
(b) SUBJECT MATTER JURISDICTION	Power Of A Court To Hear If: Complete Diversity	Action brought in Federal District court in State B Subject matter jurisdiction based on diversity S citizen of State S/B citizen of State B	
	Amount In Controversy	Contract price as written $80,000 B brought action against S for reformation of the contract/alleged price was $60,000 $80,000 figure in contract was a typographical error S counterclaimed for $80,000 purchase price set forth in the contract	Subject Matter Jurisdiction Arguably Present

(2) COURT'S RULING ON MOTION TO STRIKE DEMAND FOR JURY TRIAL

(I)	(R)	(A)	(C)
RIGHT TO JURY TRIAL	7th Amendment Permits Jury Trials for Legal Issues/Not Equitable Issues	B brought action against S for reformation of the contract price (equitable?) S counterclaimed for the $80,000 purchase price set forth in contract & demanded jury trial (legal?)	Right To Jury Trial

(3) COURT'S RULING ON OBJECTION TO INTERROGATORIES

(I)	(R)	(A)	(C)
SCOPE Of DISCOVERY	Relevant To Claim/Defense Reasonably Calculated To Lead To Admissible Evidence	B alleged agreed price $60,000/$80,000 Contract price typographical error S served B with interrogatories a. Have you had Whiteacre appraised b. By whom/what values/attach written reports from all appraisers	Proper Scope of Discovery
INTERROGATORIES	Written Questions Submitted To Party Written Answers On Information/Belief	B brought an action against S S served B with interrogatories S demanded responses to following a. Have you had Whiteacre appraised b. By whom/what values/attach written reports from all appraisers	Proper Device
EXPERT TESTIMONY (Pre-12/93)	Experts Retained For Non-litigation Purpose-No Protection	B alleged agreed price $60,000 Appraised value of Whiteacre Interrogatories who/what /attach reports At trial., appraiser on behalf of B that value of Whiteacre $63,200 supra	No Protection
	Experts Retained For Litigation Purpose-Qualified Privilege	B alleged agreed price $60,000 Appraised value of Whiteacre Interrogatories who/what /attach reports At trial, appraiser on behalf of B that value of Whiteacre $63,200 supra	Qualified Privilege

(I)	(R)	(A)	(C)
EXPERT TESTIMONY (Post-12/93)	Parties Must Automatically Disclose Expert Testimony	B alleged agreed price $60,000 Appraised value of Whiteacre Interrogatories who/what /attach reports At trial. appraiser on behalf of B that value of Whiteacre $63,200 supra	Arguable
	Disclosure Must Include Testimony/Reports	Attach reports supra	

(4) COURT'S RULING IN GRANTING THE RENEWED MOTION FOR A JUDGMENT AS A MATTER OF LAW

(I)	(R)	(A)	(C)
RENEWED MOTION FOR A JUDGMENT AS A MATTER OF LAW	Request for Court To Set Aside Jury Verdict As A Matter of Law	Jury returned verdict for S for $80,000/judgment entered accordingly/B moved for renewed motion or new trial Court granted	Improper Ruling
	Trial Evidence Insufficient To Support Verdict	B testified agreed price $60,000/$80,000 contract price typographical error B's appraiser testified value $63,200 supra S testified agreed price $80,000/contract provided $80,000 price (reasonable jury verdict?)	

(5) PROCEDURAL ARGUMENTS BY S IN OPPOSITION THE TO RENEWED MOTION FOR A JUDGMENT AS A MATTER OF LAW

(I)	(R)	(A)	(C)
RENEWED MOTION FOR A JUDGMENT AS A MATTER OF LAW	Moving Party Must 1st Make A Motion For A Judgment As A Matter Of Law/New Trial As A Matter of Law	Jury returned verdict for S supra Judgment entered on that verdict accordingly B promptly moved for motion or a new trial	Improper Ruling
	Opposing Party Must Have Been Fully Heard On Motion's Material Issues	B did not move for judgment as a matter of law on the issue of the purchase price	

<u>**EXAMPLE OF IRAC CIVIL PROCEDURE ISSUE**</u>

(I) <u>**Scope of Discovery**</u>

(R) Discovery may inquire into all non-privileged information that is (1) <u>relevant</u> to the <u>claim</u> or <u>defense</u> of <u>any</u> <u>party</u> which is (2) <u>reasonably</u> <u>calculated</u> to <u>lead</u> to the discovery of <u>admissible</u> <u>evidence</u> even though such evidence may not be admissible at trial.

(A) Byer has alleged that the agreed purchase price of the land was $60,000. Byer was preparing to present evidence by an appraiser concerning the actual value of Whiteacre at the time Buyer and Seler signed the contract. <u>Appraisal</u> evidence would be (1) <u>relevant</u> to the Buyer's <u>claim</u> regarding the agreed upon purchase <u>price</u> because it would determine Whiteacre's value at the time of contracting.

This evidence would be (2) r<u>easonably</u> <u>calculated</u> to <u>lead</u> to further <u>admissible</u> <u>evidence</u> concerning Byer's belief in the value of the land and whether he agreed to pay $60,000.00 or $80,000.00 at the time he signed the contract.

(C) Therefore, Seler's interrogatories were within the scope of discovery.

SUGGESTED MODEL ANSWER

BYER v. SELER

1. COURT'S RULING ON THE MOTION TO DISMISS

a. Personal Jurisdiction

Personal jurisdiction is the power of the court to render a judgment that binds a defendant personally.

Since Byer served Seler pursuant to a long arm statute, Byer is attempting to invoke personal jurisdiction over Seler.

Long Arm Statute

A long arm statute is a state statute which authorizes the courts of that state to exercise personal jurisdiction over non-residents by serving non-residents with process outside of the forum state. A federal court is bound, under F.R.C.P. 4, to apply the long arm statute of the state within which it sits.

Seler is a State S citizen. Seler is a nonresident of State B and is outside of the forum state. However, State B will enforce service of process on Seler by exercising personal jurisdiction over him through the State B long arm statute.

1) Does the Transaction Fall Within the Long Arm Statute?

Long arm statutes will apply if the tortious act occurred in the forum. Liberal long-arm statutes permit the exercise of jurisdiction irrespective of where the harm occurs. More conservative statutes allow jurisdiction only where the harm occurred within the forum.

The facts do not state the terms of the long-arm statute. Seler and Byer met in State B where they entered into a signed, written land sales contract for the sale of Whiteacre located in State W. The contract document, signed by both, contained an alleged typographical error concerning the price. The price discrepancy arose in State B. Under both liberal and conservative long-arm statutes, State B, is the forum wherein the harm occurred.

Assuming the terms of the statute authorize the court to exercise personal jurisdiction over Seler, the exercise of personal jurisdiction over Seler must not violate Seler's rights under the Due Process Clause of the U.S. Constitution.

2) Due Process - Minimum Contacts

Under the case of **International Shoe**, the court may exercise jurisdiction over a defendant who is not present in the forum state only if that defendant has minimum contacts with the forum state such that the maintenance of the suit does not offend traditional notions of fair play and substantial justice.

As previously established, Seler is a State B nonresident defendant. He met Byer in State B where they both signed a written agreement for the sale of Whiteacre. Seler then returned to State S where he sent a deed conveying good title to Whiteacre to Byer in State B. By going to State B to contract with Byer, Seler deliberately transacted business in State B and relied of State B contract law while doing so.

Seler followed up this initial contact in State B by returning to State S where he then sent the deed to Buyer who was in State B. This further action demonstrated ongoing deliberate conduct directed at State B. By entering the forum state to form a contract and then sending the deed in follow-up, Seler should have reasonably known that he was reaching into the forum state to purposefully avail himself of the economic benefits and protections of State B's contract law (**Burger King.**) Seler has sufficient contacts in State B to allow it to exercise jurisdiction over him.

Seler will counter that he had only one meeting in State B. Sending the deed to Byer in State B was incidental to the original meeting. Such an act did not constitute a sufficient quantity of contacts necessary to subject Seler to the burdens associated with doing business in that forum. Furthermore, Byer's suit arises out of a contract for the sale of land and the land is located in State W, not State B. Thus, Seler should reasonably expect to be sued in State W, not State B.

However, Seler actively transacted business in State B. Byer's cause of action for reformation directly arises out of the contract signed by Seler in State B. State B has a strong interest in opening its courts to its own citizens and protecting its citizens from fraud or mistakes in drafting contracts. Contract disputes are always foreseeable. Seler should have reasonably expected to be sued in State B if a contract dispute arose.

Seler's contact in State B constitutes sufficient minimum contacts such that the maintenance of the suit in that jurisdiction does not offend traditional notions of fair play and substantial justice for purposes of litigation fairness.

Notice - Service of Process

The defendant must receive service of process allowing notice reasonably calculated to apprise it of the pendency of the action and an opportunity to be heard sufficient to satisfy the requirements of constitutional procedural due process (**Mullane.**)

The facts indicate that personal jurisdiction over Seler was based on service of process executed on Seler in State S under the State B long arm statute. Assuming that it was properly done, Seler has been given notice reasonably calculated to apprise him of the pendency of Byer's action against him and an opportunity to present any objection to the service of process that will be heard in the court in which the action was filed.

Service of process executed on Seler under the State B long arm statute is sufficient to satisfy the requirements of constitutional procedural due process.

Therefore, State B may exercise personal jurisdiction over Seler. The court's ruling was proper.

b. Subject Matter Jurisdiction - Diversity

A federal court has the power to hear and determine a particular type of controversy if complete diversity exists between the plaintiff and defendant and the amount in controversy exceeds $75,000 exclusive of interest and costs.

Byer filed suit in federal district court in State B. Seler was a citizen of State S. Byer was a citizen of State B. Therefore, because no defendant is a citizen of the same state as any plaintiff, there is complete diversity among the parties.

Byer has alleged a $60,000 contract price. He seeks to reform the contract to reflect that price. If the court reforms the contract as requested by Byer, the value to Byer will be $20,000 which is the difference between the $80,000 price stated in the contract and the reformed price of $60,000. Seler will argue that this amount does not satisfy the minimum $75,000 amount in controversy requirement.

However, a court might be amenable to the following argument. Since Seler performed his side of the bargain by delivering the deed to Whiteacre, but Byer did not perform his obligation by delivering the stated purchase price, Seler, not Byer, would normally be the plaintiff in an action for the purchase price. In such an action, the amount in controversy would have been $80,000 and Byer, as defendant, would have counterclaimed for reformation to reduce the price to $60,000. In such a case, the federal court would clearly have had diversity jurisdiction. Why should the fact that Byer "jumped the gun" divest the court of diversity jurisdiction and deprive Seler of the opportunity to have the matter heard in federal court? The issue is still the agreed purchase price: $80,000 or $60,000?

The federal court may have proper subject matter jurisdiction. The court's ruling was proper.

2. COURT'S RULING ON THE MOTION TO STRIKE THE DEMAND FOR THE JURY TRIAL

7th Amendment - Right to a Jury Trial

The 7th Amendment guarantees a right to a jury trial for all legal actions triable at common law in excess of $20.00. There is no similar right to a jury trial of equitable claims.

Byer has brought an action against Seler for reformation of the contract price. Reformation is an action in equity for which no jury trial would normally be granted.

However, Seler has counterclaim for $80,000 in damages which raises a legal issue. The contract price dispute involves a common issue shared by both the legal and equitable claims. Seler must not be deprived of his 7th Amendment right to have that common legal issue tried by a jury. Therefore, all issues relating to Seler's counterclaim related to his legal right to damages must be tried first by a jury. Any remaining equitable issues, including Buyer's claim for reformation, will be tried by a judge (**Beacon Theatres.**)

Seler has a right to a jury trial. The court's ruling was proper.

3. COURT'S RULING ON THE OBJECTION TO THE INTERROGATORIES

Scope of Discovery

Scope of Discovery

Discovery may inquire into all non-privileged information that is relevant to the claim or defense of any party which is reasonably calculated to lead to the discovery of admissible evidence even though such evidence may not be admissible at trial.

Byer has alleged that the agreed purchase price of the land was $60,000. Byer was preparing to present evidence by an appraiser concerning the actual value of Whiteacre at the time Buyer and Seler signed the contract. Appraisal evidence would be relevant to the Buyer's claim regarding the agreed upon purchase price because it would determine Whiteacre's value at the time of contracting.

This evidence would be reasonably calculated to lead to further admissible evidence concerning Byer's belief in the value of the land and whether he agreed to pay $60,000.00 or $80,000.00 at the time he signed the contract.

Therefore, Seler's interrogatories were within the scope of discovery.

Discovery Device - Interrogatory

Interrogatories are discovery devices in the form of written questions submitted to a party of a lawsuit requiring written responses based on information and belief.

The facts stipulate that Seler served Byer with interrogatories which are a set of written questions. Because Byer brought an action against Seler and was a party to the lawsuit, this was an appropriate use of this written discovery device. The questions submitted demanded responses to whether Byer had Whiteacre appraised, by whom, at what value, and further asked for attached copies from all appraisers. Byer's responses to these questions could be compelled based on Byer's information and belief.

The interrogatories were a proper discovery device.

Expert Testimony - Pre December 1993 Amendments

Under Rule 26(b)(4) as it existed prior to the December 1993 amendments of the Federal Rules, if experts are retained for a non-litigation purpose, any reports developed for this non-litigation purpose would received no protection from discovery. However, if experts are retained in anticipation of litigation or for trial, any facts and opinions acquired by these appraisers for litigation purposes would receive qualified immunity from discovery.

Byer engaged he services of appraisers to support Byer's position that he agreed to pay $60,000 for Whiteacre which was not worth more than $63,200 at the time Byer signed the land sales contract. However, the facts do not clearly indicate when Byer hired his appraisers or for what purpose he hired them. If Byer retained appraisers to appraise the value of Whiteacre to help in his negotiations with Seler, any appraisals developed for this non-litigation purpose would receive no protection from discovery even if these appraisers were later retained by Byer to testify on his behalf at trial.

However, if Byer retained these appraisers in anticipation of litigation or for trial, any facts and opinions acquired from them for litigation purposes would receive qualified immunity from discovery.

If Byer's experts were retained by Byer in anticipation of litigation, but not designated to testify as expert witnesses, Seler would have to make a motion and prove the existence of exceptional circumstances to compel production of appraisal reports and/or depositions of the appraisers.

It appears that Byer undoubtedly hired the appraisers for use as experts at trial. If any of these appraisers had been designated to testify for Byer as expert witnesses, Seler would be entitled to discover their identity and the substance of the facts and opinions upon which they would testify. Thus, even if Byer's appraisers were hired in anticipation of litigation, Seler could compel Byer to identify them and disclose the facts upon which their appraised values were based.

As to Seler's request for copies of all written reports received by Byer from his appraisers, if the reports were compiled in anticipation of litigation, such documents are deemed expert reports. They contain facts and opinions developed for use in preparing Byer's case for trial. Therefore, the written reports are protected by a qualified privilege and may not be compelled by Seler.

Expert Testimony - Post December 1993 Amendments

Rule 26(a) now requires all parties to automatically disclose all persons who may offer expert testimony on their behalf at trial without waiting for any discovery demand. Disclosure must also include detailed reports by any expert witnesses retained or specially employed by any party to provide testimony at trial or whose duties as that party's employee regularly involves giving expert testimony. Rule 26(b)(4) now no longer gives any protection to the facts and opinions of expert witnesses even if acquired or developed in anticipation of litigation.

Regarding the identity and the facts and opinions of any appraisers who acquired or developed such information for non-litigation purposes, the result is the same as in the pre-December 1993 discussion. Such information receives no protection from discovery. Regarding the identity and the facts and opinions of any appraisers retained or specially employed by Byer in anticipation of litigation, but not to provide trial testimony, the results are the same as discussed in the pre-December 1993 discussion.

If the appraisers were hired as experts by Byer to offer testimony at trial, Byer must automatically disclose the identity of all these persons and the facts and opinions of these expert witnesses even if acquired or developed in anticipation of litigation. This disclosure must also include any written appraisals received from all appraisers because disclosure must also include detailed reports by any expert witnesses retained or specially employed by any party to provide testimony at trial or whose duties as that party's employee regularly involves giving expert testimony.

Therefore, the first interrogatory, asking: "Have you had Whiteacre appraised?" is not protected by any rule and is not objectionable. The interrogatories requesting the names of the appraisers and the appraised value or values are not objectionable either. The request for written reports is also proper.

4. COURT'S RULING IN GRANTING THE RENEWED MOTION FOR A JUDGMENT AS A MATTER OF LAW

A renewed motion for a judgment as a matter of law, previously known as a judgment notwithstanding the verdict, is a request for the court to set aside the jury verdict and to enter a judgment for the party that lost the verdict. The court can grant this motion only if, as a matter of law (not discretion), the evidence presented at trial is rationally insufficient to support the jury verdict.

The court granted Byer's renewed motion for a judgment as a matter of law. This acted to nullify Seler's $80,000 judgment returned by the jury. The court must have believed the jury's verdict for Seler in the amount of $80,000 was rationally insufficient based upon the evidence presented at trial.

Seler will contend that, although Byer testified that the agreed price was $60,000, the jury is free to disbelieve the testimony of Byer. Credibility of witnesses is an issue for the jury to determine. This is particularly true where, as here, Byer has a direct interest in the outcome of the case.

Further, Byer admitted testimony by his appraiser that Whiteacre was worth $63,200 at most when the contract was signed. However, such evidence is not conclusive of the price Byer originally agreed to pay. The fact that Byer's expert appraised Whiteacre at $63,200 carries with it many interpretations. Byer's appraiser was not a witness to the Byer/Seler contract negotiations for Whiteacre. He did not corroborate Byer's testimony that the agreed price was $60,000. He merely offered his opinion as to the value of Whiteacre at the time the contract was signed.

Even if the jury believed the appraiser's testimony, a reasonable jury could have decided that the appraiser's testimony only proved the value of Whiteacre, not what Byer had agreed to pay for it.

Byer's expert testimony must be considered in light of all the evidence presented by both parties. The jury is not bound to decide the facts based solely on the expert appraisal.

Seler testified that the agreed price was $80,000. This testimony was corroborated by the contract document stipulating a $80,000 price signed by both Byer and Seler. In this battle of credibility between Byer and Seler, the jury was free to believe Seler and not Byer. Seler's evidence appears much more compelling in light of the signatures appearing on the contract.

If the jury considered all evidence and chose to believe that Seler's testimony was rationally supported by evidence more compelling than Byer's, it was reasonable for it to enter a $80,000 verdict for Seler. The court has no discretion to overturn the jury's verdict on a renewed motion for judgment as a matter of law merely because he disagrees with the jury's findings. In this case, there was sufficient evidence to rationally support a verdict for either party.

The court abused its discretion and committed an error of law by granting Byer's motion. The court's ruling was improper.

[NOTE: The facts do not indicate how the court ruled, if at all, on Byer's alternative motion for a new trial. The call of the question does not ask for a discussion regarding Byer's new trial motion. Under Rule 50, even though the court granted Byer's renewed motion for a judgment as a matter of law, it would also have to conditionally rule on Byer's alternative new trial motion in case the court's ruling on the judgment as a matter of law is reversed on appeal.]

5. PROCEDURAL ARGUMENT IN OPPOSITION TO THE RENEWED MOTION FOR A JUDGMENT AS A MATTER OF LAW

Under Rule 50, a renewed motion for a judgment as a matter of law cannot be considered unless the moving party has previously made a motion for a judgment as a matter of law on the same material issue before the close of all the evidence. The earliest a party can move for a judgment as a matter of law is after the opposing party has been fully heard on the material issue that is the subject of the motion.

After the jury returned a verdict for Seler and the judgment was entered on that verdict, Byer promptly moved for a renewed motion for judgment as a matter of law or a new trial. However, prior to the close of the evidence, Byer did not move for a judgment as a matter of law on the issue of the agreed purchase price, the material issue that was the subject of the motion.

Byer's motion is procedurally improper. Seler should have opposed Byer's motion on this procedural basis.

CIVIL PROCEDURE QUESTION #3

PLAINTIFFS v. APOW

APOW owns and operates a nuclear power plant. For one hour on each of the three successive days, the plant emitted heavy radiation over the surrounding area which has a population of 10,000 persons. Several individuals injured by the radiation emitted on the third day brought a class action for damages in an appropriate federal district court against APOW on behalf of all those injured on one or more of the three days. After describing the relevant facts, the complaint alleged only that APOW was responsible for "wrongful conduct." Jurisdiction was based properly and exclusively on diversity of citizenship.

1. APOW moved to dismiss the complaint for failure to state a claim upon which relief could be granted. The motion was denied.

2. APOW then opposed plaintiffs' motion to certify the class, arguing that there was no common issue and the plaintiffs' claims were not typical of the class. Certification was granted.

3. During discovery, plaintiffs requested that APOW produce a memorandum concerning possible legal liability for nuclear power accidents prepared by APOW's legal staff prior to the accident but following minor accidents at another company's nuclear power plant. APOW objected. The state in which the action was brought had abolished its own work product doctrine a year earlier. The court held that the memorandum could be discovered.

Was each of the court's rulings correct? Discuss.

IRAC OUTLINE SHEET

(I)	(R)	(A)	(C)

EXAMPLE OF PROPER IRAC OUTLINE

(1) APOW'S MOTION TO DISMISS

(I)	(R)	(A)	(C)
SUFFICIENCY OF THE COMPLAINT	Federal Notice Pleading Short/Plain Statement Showing Plaintiff Entitled To Relief	APOW owns & operates a nuclear plant For one hour on each of 3 successive days, the plant emitted heavy radiation over surrounding area Class action for damages in an appropriate federal district court against APOW Described relevant facts/alleged only that APOW was responsible for "wrongful conduct"	Complaint Sufficient Under Federal Rules Motion Properly Denied
	State Code Pleading Statement Of Ultimate Facts	Wrongful conduct (Too vague/conclusory?)	

(2) APOW'S OPPOSITION TO PLAINTIFFS' MOTION TO CERTIFY CLASS

(I)	(R)	(A)	(C)
CLASS ACTION	Ascertainable Class	Plaintiffs' motion to certify the class of those injured on one of three days	
	Class Representative Is A Member	Several individuals injured...brought class action A motion to certify class was filed by Plaintiffs' representative	
	Numerosity	APOW owns/operates a nuclear plant Radiation over surrounding areas/population 10,000 persons	Proper Class Action
	Commonality of Law/Fact	For one hour on each of 3 successive days, radiation over surrounding area "Wrongful conduct"	
	Typicality Claims/Defenses	Several individuals injured on 3rd day brought action on behalf of all those injured on one or more of the 3 days	
	Adequate Representation	Several individuals injured on 3rd day brought action on behalf of all those injured on one	
	Class Action: 3 Required Categories	Several individuals injured on 3rd day brought action supra (Damage category)	

(3) PLAINTIFFS' REQUEST FOR APOW'S MEMORANDUM

(I)	(R)	(A)	(C)
CHOICE OF LAW	ERIE Doctrine Requires Federal Court In Diversity	Federal district court/jurisdiction based properly & exclusively on diversity of citizenship	Federal Rule Controls
	Apply State Substantive/Federal Procedural Law Where Federal Law On Point	The state in which the action was brought had abolished its own work product doctrine a year earlier (work product-procedural)	
SCOPE OF DISCOVERY	Relevant To Claim/Defense	During discovery, plaintiffs' requested that APOW produce a memo concerning possible legal liability for nuclear power accidents	Proper Scope Of Discovery
	Reasonably Calculated To Lead To Admissible Evidence	A memo concerning possible legal liability for nuclear power accidents supra Court held that the memo could be discovered	
EXCEPTION - WORK PRODUCT	Qualified Privilege Exists If: Materials Prepared By Party/Attorney Or Staff	Possible legal liability Memo prepared by APOW's legal staff prior to the accident but following minor accidents at another company's nuclear plant	Arguable
	Anticipation Of Litigation	Possible legal liability	
	Substantial Need	No facts	
	Mental Impressions	Supra	
	Extreme Necessity	Supra	

EXAMPLE OF IRAC CIVIL PROCEDURE ISSUE

(I) **Choice of Law**

(R) Under the **Erie Doctrine**, a federal court sitting in diversity must apply (1) state substantive law but need not apply state procedural law where there exists a (2) federal rule of civil procedure that is on point. In this instance, the Supremacy Clause of the U.S. Constitution requires that the federal procedural rule must be applied over any conflicting state rule of procedure (**Hanna.**)

(A) Plaintiffs brought their claim in federal district court with jurisdiction properly and exclusively based on diversity of citizenship. In such a case, (1) controlling substantive rules are derived entirely from state law.

The state in which the action was brought had abolished its own work product doctrine a year earlier. In the absence of a state law controlling the substantive issue of work product, (2) the federal law recognizes work product practice and procedure, is on point, and will predominate.

The state discovery rules are clearly in conflict with Rule 26(b)(3) because state law would require production of work product that might be protected from discovery under the federal rules. Thus, the application of state discovery rules would undermine a valid federal rule of civil procedure and thereby violate the Supremacy Clause. Therefore, the federal court must apply F.R.C.P. 26(b)(3) to resolve the work product issue.

(C) Choice of law will be governed by the federal rules.

SUGGESTED MODEL ANSWER

1. APOW'S MOTION TO DISMISS THE COMPLAINT

Sufficiency of the Complaint

Rule 8(a) of the federal rules require that a complaint contains a short, plain statement of the claim sufficient to show that the pleader is entitled to relief. State code pleading requires an allegation of ultimate facts of the cause of action with particularity.

APOW owns and operates a nuclear plant. As a result of its plant operation, the plant emitted heavy radiation over the surrounding area for one hour on each of three successive days. Plaintiffs filed a class action against APOW for damages in the appropriate federal district court. The complaint described the relevant facts concerning APOW's emission of heavy radiation over the surrounding area where the plaintiffs live. These short, plain statements of the claim alleging APOW's responsibility for "wrongful conduct" were sufficient to show that the plaintiffs were entitled to relief.

APOW will assert that the allegation of "wrongful conduct" was an insufficient statement of the claim to show that the plaintiffs are entitled to relief as a result of APOW's plant operation.

However, the purpose of the federal rules is simply to identify the transaction from which the plaintiffs' claim arises. Their statement of the relevant facts regarding the heavy radiation emission on the designated three days coupled with the allegation of "wrongful conduct" would be sufficient to put APOW on notice of the basis of the claim. Under notice pleading, the complaint need only notify the defendant of the underlying transaction which gives rise to the lawsuit, not the particular facts or legal theories that support plaintiff's case. Therefore, the lack of precision in identifying a specific cause of action would not be necessary.

Even in liberal state code pleading jurisdictions, a statement of the relevant facts concerning the heavy radiation emission on the specified three days coupled with the allegation of "wrongful conduct" would be regarded as an allegation of ultimate facts of the cause of action. Such ordinary and precise language provides sufficient facts with particularity to constitute a cause of action.

APOW may rebut that "wrongful conduct" is vague and too general. Such language should be regarded as surplusage and should be deemed a conclusion rather than a sufficient notice of the underlying incident which gives rise to the class action suit against it.

However, the court must sustain the complaint as long as there is some legal theory, recognized under the applicable law, which affords the plaintiff some form of relief. Although not specifically pleaded, the allegations based on the relevant facts concerning the radiation emissions seems a sufficient statement of the ultimate facts giving rise to a cause of action in tort for wrongful conduct.

Plaintiff's complaint is sufficient under the federal rules. The court properly denied APOW's motion to dismiss.

2. APOW'S OPPOSITION TO PLAINTIFFS' MOTION TO CERTIFY THE CLASS

Class Action

Under the federal rules, the court may exercise its discretion to certify an action as a class action where there is an ascertainable class, the class representative(s) is a member of that class, numerosity of class members is present, commonality exists as to questions of law or fact, typicality exists as to claims or defenses, there is adequate representation of the class, and the class action falls within at least one of the three categories of federal class actions which includes Prejudice, Injunctive or Damage class actions.

The complaint describes all those injured on one or more of the three days. Anyone who was injured by the emission during one or more of the three days is in the class. Anyone who wasn't injured during one or more of the three days is not. This description identifies an ascertainable class.

However, defendant APOW might raise some of the following questions to challenge the adequacy of this class description. Who lives in the "surrounding area"? What territory does it include? Was every resident in this area contaminated? Are they all class members? Must they all be sent notice? The facts stipulate that the class representatives themselves were injured only on the third day of emissions. This makes it likely that some residents were not exposed or injured on any of the three days. Further, the effects of radiation exposure are often not apparent for many years. What about those persons who do not become sick many years after the incident in question? Are they members of this "class"? The likely outcome is that the court will require that notice be sent to everyone residing or working within the area of contamination.

Several individuals injured by the radiation emitted on the third day brought a class action for damages. Assuming the class consists of all persons affected by the radiation on any of the three days, the class representatives would be members of the class.

A motion to certify the plaintiffs' class was filed by plaintiffs' representatives who alleged that the radiation emitted by APOW's nuclear plant spread over a surrounding area where 10,000 persons resided. There is a strong likelihood that the majority of the 10,000 persons exposed to the radiation would bring suit. Each person in the affected area could easily be individually notified of the action. Joinder of all of these as named plaintiffs would be impracticable. Therefore, numerosity of plaintiffs exists.

The emission of radiation for one hour on each of three succeeding days over the surrounding area where the population was affected was a common nucleus of fact upon which APOW's liability would be determined. Further, APOW's wrongful conduct of allowing such emissions would be based on the relevant law giving the basis for negligence or intentional torts governing such actions. Since the plaintiffs' claims involve both common questions of law and fact, APOW's allegation that each plaintiff's damages may vary will not defeat their claims.

APOW will rebut that the plaintiffs' representatives were allegedly injured only on the third day of the radiation emission. Therefore, their injuries were not typical of the remaining persons who would allege injuries on the other two days of radiation emission.

However, it does not appear that the day upon which potential plaintiffs sustained injury is determinative of typicality. What is more compelling is that all plaintiffs were cumulatively injured during the three days when the radiation was being emitted. Since the plaintiffs bringing suit alleged specific injury to themselves and others, they would be motivated to protect the cumulative rights of all persons who were injured during any part of the three days of radiation emission. Therefore, the claims for relief from APOW's wrongful conduct would be typical to all plaintiffs.

Finally, the plaintiffs' representatives are alleging injuries from the radiation emission both to themselves and others. The representatives' own interests coincide with that of the class members. The similarity of claims for the entire class would ensure that the representatives would be motivated to vigorously litigate their own personal claims and those of the class. Thus, adequate representation for all plaintiffs who were radiation exposure victims could be assured.

The issue that the members of the class have in common is that they all claim to have been injured in a similar way and the primary remedy sought is damages. The only category of class action that would apply would be the damage class action. In order to certify this action as a damage class action, the court must find that proceeding as a class action is superior to any alternative means of enforcing the claims of the class members and that the common questions of law and fact shared by the class members predominate over the questions that divide them.

Courts do not favor class action treatment for "mass tort" cases such as this. First, if heavy exposure to radiation over a three-day period has caused severe injuries to many class members, these persons may have a strong interest in independently pursuing their own claims in separate lawsuits. If this is true, the class members are already "empowered" by the size of their individual claims and do not need to rely on a class action to enforce their rights (**Dalkon Shield.**)

Second, a class action may not promote judicial economy in this case because there may be many issues that divide the class. In addition to the wide variety of injuries that radiation exposure can cause, the question of causation can differ on an individual basis. For example, each individual must surely have been exposed to differing levels of radiation depending on the distance from the nuclear plant and the duration and frequency of exposure.

Also, each individual must establish that his injury was proximately caused by the radiation leak in question and not by some prior exposure to radiation, or to some other cause in fact.

On the other hand, the class action could be limited to determining whether the emissions occurred and the causation of the leakage.

The court was correct in granting plaintiffs' motion for certification of the class.

3. PLAINTIFFS' REQUEST FOR APOW'S MEMORANDUM

Choice of Law

Under the **Erie Doctrine**, a federal court sitting in diversity must apply state substantive law but need not apply state procedural law where there exists a federal rule of civil procedure that is on point. In this instance, the Supremacy Clause of the U.S. Constitution requires that the federal procedural rule must be applied over any conflicting state rule of procedure (**Hanna.**)

Plaintiffs brought their claim in federal district court with jurisdiction properly and exclusively based on diversity of citizenship. In such a case, controlling substantive rules are derived entirely from state law.

The state in which the action was brought had abolished its own work product doctrine a year earlier. In the absence of a state law controlling the substantive issue of work product, the federal law recognizes work product practice and procedure, is on point, and will predominate.

The state discovery rules are clearly in conflict with Rule 26(b)(3) because state law would require production of work product that might be protected from discovery under the federal rules. Thus, the application of state discovery rules would undermine a valid federal rule of civil procedure and thereby violate the Supremacy Clause. Therefore, the federal court must apply F.R.C.P. 26(b)(3) to resolve the work product issue.

Choice of law will be governed by the federal rules.

Scope of Discovery

Discovery may inquire into all non-privileged information that is relevant to the claim or defense of any party which is reasonably calculated to lead to the discovery of admissible evidence even though such evidence may not be admissible at trial.

The discovery request for an APOW memo concerning possible legal liability for nuclear power accidents that was prepared by APOW's legal staff following minor accidents at another company's nuclear power plan is non-privileged and relevant to plaintiffs' claim concerning APOW's wrongful conduct alleged in the complaint. The memo may contain facts regarding potential problems at APOW's nuclear plant which could cause accidents and create legal liability for APOW. It might indicate an awareness by APOW of the types of hazards generally inherent in the operations of nuclear power plants that should have caused APOW to look for, detect, and correct the defect that caused the radiation emissions.

The information contained in the memo is reasonably calculated to lead to further discoverable admissible evidence concerning APOW's knowledge of the types of hazards inherent in the operations of their nuclear plant that may have been prevented absent APOW's "wrongful conduct."

Therefore, the memo falls within the scope of discovery.

Exception - Work Product

Pursuant to the court's decision in **Hickman v. Taylor**, there is a qualified immunity from discovery for documents or other tangible things prepared in anticipation of litigation by or for a party or that party's representative unless the discovering party can show a substantial need and inability to obtain equivalent material by other means. The mental impressions, opinions, theories and strategies of an attorney of a party receive the highest degree of protection and cannot be discovered absent extreme necessity.

APOW will contend that the memo, i.e., document, in question was prepared by its legal staff. Although it was prepared prior to the present action, it was following minor accidents at another company's nuclear plant. The nature of that company's nuclear plant operations was similar in nature to APOW's. Thus, the information concerning possible legal liability was gathered in anticipation of litigation that could likely arise from APOW's own operations due to the inherent danger associated with nuclear plant operations.

Further, the memo contained information concerning possible legal liability. Such possibilities would be the result of mental impressions, opinions and theories by APOW's legal staff. Strategy and impressions of this nature prepared in anticipation of future claims are protected by the privilege absent extreme necessity.

Plaintiff may rebut that the report was initiated before APOW had been sued and was not prepared in anticipation of the present litigation but for legitimate ordinary, routine business purposes. There is a very strong argument that the purpose for preparing this memorandum was to avoid or prevent future liability and future lawsuits and, thus, save lives and save APOW a lot of money in legal fees and judgments. The purpose of preventing potential lawsuits by making sure APOW is in compliance with legal standards is very different from anticipating litigation and preparing to fight it. Work product immunity protects only materials prepared to fight, or litigate an anticipated lawsuit, not to prevent one.

Plaintiffs may argue that APOW's motivation in requesting its legal department to prepare this memorandum was concern about avoiding potential legal liability prompted by liability incurred by other nuclear power companies.

On other hand, if APOW's purpose in preparing the memorandum was not to prevent the inevitable lawsuits which arise out of nonpreventable accidents inherent in running nuclear power plants, but rather, to plan ahead to prepare in advance to fight such suits, the memorandum might fall within the protection of the work product rule.

Further, APOW would contend that the plaintiffs could conduct their own investigation into accidents involving other companies' nuclear plant accidents and can demonstrate no substantial need and inability to obtain equivalent material by other means. .

However, the memo indicates that, before the incident in question, APOW knew of the potential danger of radiation leaks. Plaintiffs would have a substantial need for this type of powerful evidence and they could not obtain the equivalent of this evidence through their own after-the-fact investigation.

That portion of the memo which assesses “possible legal liability for nuclear accidents” are legal opinions and theories and the lawyers' thought processes that constitute the more protected type of work product known as mental impressions. Mental impressions are discoverable only in rare cases such as where they constitute crucial and the only evidence in a case. This does not appear to be the case in this instance Therefore, this portion of the memo may be protected. However, the remainder of the memo is not privileged work product.

Therefore, the court's ruling was proper.

CIVIL PROCEDURE QUESTION #4

PAUL v. CONCO/MANCO

Paul was injured while operating a drill press manufactured by Manco, a wholly-owned corporate subsidiary of Conco, a corporation. Three days before the statute of limitations ran, Paul filed suit in federal district court in State X against Conco. Service of process was made the same day on the named defendant. One week later, Paul moved to add Manco as a defendant and the motion was granted.

Prior to trial, Paul sought discovery of a report that had been made to Manco by Brown, an investigator for Manco, who had inspected the machine and the circumstances of the accident immediately thereafter. The trial court ordered a copy of Brown's report delivered to Paul's attorney.

In selecting the jury, the judge conducted the voir dire, but refused the defendants' request that the judge ask the members of the jury panel whether any of them would be prejudiced against corporations in reaching a verdict. A verdict was returned in favor of plaintiff and against both defendants for $75,000 damages.

Both defendants moved for a new trial. The trial judge granted a new trial on the issue of damages alone, unless plaintiff agreed to a reduction in the verdict from $75,000 to $25,000. Plaintiff agreed to the reduction under protest. Both defendants appeal, asserting as error the trial court's action in

(1) adding Manco as a party defendant,

(2) ordering discovery of Brown's report,

(3) refusing to ask prospective jurors whether, in reaching a verdict, they would be prejudiced against corporations.

Plaintiff cross-appealed, asserting as error the trial court's order granting a new trial unless plaintiff accepted a reduction in the verdict from $75,000 to $25,000.

How should the appellate court decide each of the above asserted errors. Discuss.

IRAC OUTLINE SHEET

(I)	(R)	(A)	(C)

EXAMPLE OF PROPER IRAC OUTLINE

PAUL v. CONCO (C) AND MANCO (M):

ADDING MANCO AS A DEFENDANT:

(I)	(R)	(A)	(C)
AMENDMENT OF COMPLAINT BY ADDING PARTY	Federal Rules: One Amendment As A Matter of Right	Paul injured by drill press manufactured by M - wholly owned corporate subsidiary of C Filed suit in federal district court in State X & served C 3 days prior to Statute of Limitations	Amendment Valid
	Before 20 days/Before Responsive Pleading	One week later Paul moves to add M M wholly owned subsidiary of C	
DOCTRINE OF RELATION BACK-STATUTE OF LIMITATIONS	Misnomer (Mistake)	Conco, not Manco	No Relation Back Permitted
	Relates Back To The Time Initial Complaint Filed	Supra	
	Actual Notice	M sent its investigator to scene immediately after accident M a subsidiary of C Service of process on C	
	Knows/Should Have Known	M a wholly owned corporate subsidiary of C/Filing & service of process the same day on C	

DISCOVERY OF BROWN'S REPORT

(I)	(R)	(A)	(C)
SCOPE OF DISCOVERY	Relevant To Claim/Defense	Report by M's investigator immediately after accident Circumstances of accident	Proper Scope of Discovery
	Reasonably Calculated To Lead To Admissible Evidence	See facts above	
EXCEPTION: WORK PRODUCT	Qualified Privilege Exists If:		
	Materials Prepared By Party/Attorneys Or Staff	Report prepared by M's investigator Report of accident, inspection of machine & circumstances immediately after accident	Discoverable Work Product
	Anticipation Of Litigation	Report to M requested by M	
	Substantial Need	Report immediately after accident re inspection and circumstances	
	Mental Impressions	Report supra ?	
	Extreme Necessity	Report supra ?	

PREJUDICIAL VOIR DIRE

(I)	(R)	(A)	(C)
VOIR DIRE	Judge May Conduct Voir Dire	Judge conducted voir dire	
	Discretionary Absent Prejudice	Judge refused defendants' request to ask jury panel about possible prejudice to corporations in reaching a verdict Verdict returned in favor of plaintiff for $75,000 Judge reduced verdict to $25,000	Prejudicial Voir Dire If Court Erred, Remedy-Appeal

NEW TRIAL - REMITTITUR

(I)	(R)	(A)	(C)
CONDITIONAL NEW TRIAL	Judge May Order A New Trial	Trial court granted new trial unless plaintiff accept reduction in verdict from $75,000 to $25 000	Jurisdictional Split
	Conditioned Upon Plaintiff's Refusal To Accept Reduction	Plaintiff agreed under protest (split of jurisdictions)	

EXAMPLE OF IRAC CIVIL PROCEDURE ISSUE

(I) **Amendment of the Complaint by Adding a Party**

(R) F.R.C.P. 15(a) gives a party a right to (1) amend his pleading once as a matter of course at any time before the expiration of 20 days from the service of the pleading to be amended or before a responsive pleading is served.

(A) Paul was injured by a drill press manufactured by Manco, a wholly owned corporate subsidiary of co-defendant Conco. Paul filed suit in federal district court in State X and served Conco in State X three days prior to the running of the Statute of Limitations for damages resulting from his injuries. One week later, Paul (1) sought leave of the court to add Manco as a defendant. Only one week had elapsed from the date of service to the date Manco was added to the complaint which is well within the 20 days allowed. Therefore, the amendment should be allowed once as a matter of course.

Manco will rebut that allowing Paul to amend and serve Manco after the Statute of Limitations would deny it of its right to notification of litigation within the statutory period. Such a delay would impede its ability to gather evidence thereby prejudicing Manco's right to defend.

However, prejudice is not determined solely by the Statute of Limitations. The facts do not indicate that Conco had served its responsive answer to Paul's original complaint at the time that Paul sought to amend his complaint. Manco's ability to effectively defend itself would be unaffected by the running of the Statute of Limitations by four days. Since Paul has the right to amend once as a matter of course, the question of prejudice to Conco, if any, is immaterial.

(C) The court did not have discretion to prevent Paul from amending his complaint.

SUGGESTED MODEL ANSWER

PAUL v. CONCO AND MANCO

(1) ADDING MANCO AS A DEFENDANT:

Amendment of the Complaint by Adding a Party

F.R.C.P. 15(a) gives a party a right to amend his pleading once as a matter of course at any time before the expiration of 20 days from the service of the pleading to be amended or before a responsive pleading is served.

Paul was injured by a drill press manufactured by Manco, a wholly owned corporate subsidiary of co-defendant Conco. Paul filed suit in federal district court and served Conco in State X three days prior to the running of the Statute of Limitations for damages resulting from his injuries. One week later, Paul sought leave of the court to add Manco as a defendant. Only one week had elapsed from the date of service to the date Manco was added to the complaint which is well within the 20 days allowed. Therefore, the amendment should be allowed once as a matter of course.

Manco will rebut that allowing Paul to amend and serve Manco after the Statute of Limitations would deny it of its right to notification of litigation within the statutory period. Such a delay would impede its ability to gather evidence thereby prejudicing Manco's right to defend.

However, prejudice is not determined solely by the Statute of Limitations. The facts do not indicate that Conco had served its responsive answer to Paul's original complaint at the time that Paul sought to amend his complaint. Manco's ability to effectively defend itself would be unaffected by the running of the Statute of Limitations by four days. Since Paul has the right to amend once as a matter of course, the question of prejudice to Conco, if any, is immaterial.

The court did not have discretion to prevent Paul from amending his complaint.

Doctrine of Relation Back - Statute of Limitations

F.R.C.P. 15 provides that where a party has made a mistake concerning the identity of the proper defendant and seeks to amend his complaint to change the proper defendant for the improper one, that amendment will be deemed to relate back to the filing date of the original complaint if, within the period required for serving the summons and complaint, the party sought to be brought in by amendment received actual notice of the institution of the action so that he will not be prejudiced in maintaining a defense on the merits and knew or should have known that, but for a mistake concerning the identity of the proper defendant, the action would have been brought against him.

Paul originally sued Conco in federal district court and now seeks to add Manco to the lawsuit. Manco will argue that Paul did not seek to change or substitute the proper defendant for the improper defendant, but rather, to add Manco a second proper defendant. Even if Paul were unable to join Manco, the wholly-owned subsidiary of Conco who actually manufactured the drill press, it could still recover and, in fact, did recover against Conco, the parent company, who would be liable for the torts of its subsidiary. This does not seem to be a case where Paul sued the wrong defendant and now seeks to change defendants.

Paul will argue that if Conco and Manco were two parallel corporations owned by the same stockholders, and Paul mistakenly sued Conco meaning to sue Manco, his amendment would relate-back. This is supported by the fact that, immediately after the accident, Manco sent an investigator to the scene to inspect the drill press and the circumstances surrounding the accident. All this occurred before the expiration of 120 days from the filing of the original complaint against Conco.

Manco's status as a wholly owed corporate subsidiary of Conco, combined with the service of process on Conco, should have sufficiently placed Manco on actual notice of the lawsuit and the mistake in identifying the proper defendant. This notice would allow Manco to mount any appropriate defense on the merits of the action thereby eliminating any prejudice to Manco. It appears that Manco knew or should have known that, but for the mistake in suing Conco, the action would have been brought against it.

The amendment to the complaint adding Manco as a defendant may be deemed to relate back to the date Paul originally filed his complaint against Conco in State X federal court.

However, similarity of the names Manco and Conco is irrelevant under F.R.C.P. 15(c)(ii). Paul could and, in fact, did recover against Conco. A recovery against Conco would equate to a recovery against Manco, the wholly owned corporate subsidiary. The federal relation-back rule is designed to save a plaintiff from the kind of mistaken identity problem which would, otherwise, prevent him from enforcing his claim on the merits.

Therefore, the court erred in allowing Paul to add Manco.

(2) DISCOVERY OF BROWN'S REPORT:

Scope of Discovery

Discovery may inquire into all non-privileged information that is relevant to the claim or defense of any party which is reasonably calculated to lead to the discovery of admissible evidence even though such evidence may not be admissible at trial.

The report contains information concerning the inspection of the machine immediately after the accident and the circumstances of the accident. Such information is relevant to Paul's claim that he was injured while operating Manco's drill press and is reasonably calculated to lead to further admissible evidence concerning the cause of the accident.

Therefore, the report falls within the scope of discovery.

Exception: Work Product

Pursuant to the court's decision in **Hickman v. Taylor**, there is a qualified immunity from discovery for documents or other tangible things prepared in anticipation of litigation by or for a party or that party's representative unless the discovering party can show a substantial need and inability to obtain equivalent material by other means. The mental impressions, opinions, theories and strategies of an attorney of a party receive the highest degree of protection and cannot be discovered absent extreme necessity.

Manco will assert that Brown is its investigator. Manco reasonably expected Paul to file a lawsuit against Manco, the manufacturer of the drill press. Although Paul had not yet filed suit, prudent parties anticipate lawsuits. Manco would argue that it immediately dispatched Brown to gather evidence for use in defending itself in the event that Paul would file a lawsuit. It did so before the machine was repaired, before witnesses disappeared, before witness memories faded and before the accident scene was altered. Since Brown's investigation and documented reports were requested at the direction of Manco, a party defendant, in anticipation of litigation, a qualified privilege exists.

However, the report was made by Brown for Manco, not Manco's attorney. Paul will contend that, whether or not Manco anticipated a lawsuit, it would have sent Brown to investigate the accident for the ordinary, routine business purpose of preventing future accidents. Preventing future accidents serves the ordinary business purpose of increasing Manco's profits by cutting down on payments Manco might have to make in the future to injured persons or for litigation costs. Because of the immediacy of the investigation, it is more likely that the report was prepared as standard operating procedure after an accident involving Manco's drill press rather than in anticipation of litigation.

Assuming that Brown's report falls within the work product immunity, can Paul make a showing sufficient to overcome the immunity? The factual part of Brown's report is "ordinary" work product. This information goes to the very heart of his case concerning the cause of the accident. Paul's would be subjected to an undue hardship in obtaining necessary proof of liability if he were denied its access. It would be unlikely that Paul could obtain the same information or an equivalent of it a year after what Manco had obtained immediately after the accident. Therefore, Paul has a substantial need to obtain the actual report.

If the report contains Brown's opinions regarding the cause of the accident, these opinions would receive extra special protection as mental impressions work product as long as they are the mental impressions of a party's representative, not just the party's attorney. If Brown is deemed to have conducted the investigation as Manco's representative, it will be very unlikely that the court will require disclosure of that portion of the report. The court might, however, require disclosure if Paul can show extreme necessity, e.g. if the report contains an admission of Manco's culpability about which Paul has no other way of proving.

The report is not privileged work product and the court did not err in allowing its discovery.

(3) PREJUDICIAL VOIR DIRE:

Voir Dire

The judge may conduct the voir dire of the jury panel and may, at his discretion, include or exclude any questions suggested by the parties unless prejudice would result to one of the parties.

The judge conducted the voir dire of the jury, a function which is permissible both under the state and the federal rules.

However, the judge exercised his discretion when he refused Defendant's request to ask the prospective jurors questions about any prejudice they may have had against corporations in reaching a verdict. Manco and Conco will contend that as corporate defendants, they have every right to determine whether prospective jurors have such bias against corporations. Juror prejudice could adversely affect the outcome of the trial. Subsequently, such bias was demonstrated when the jury found for the plaintiff awarding him $75,000, an amount that the court itself found excessive. The court's own finding resulted in a reduction of that award to $25,000.

The question was proper in light of these facts and the judge's refusal to ask the jurors about such prejudice was an abuse of his discretion.

It appears that the court improperly refused defendant's requested voir dire. The defendant's appeal is the proper remedy for such an error.

(4) COURT'S DISPOSITION OF DEFENDANTS' NEW TRIAL MOTION

Remittitur

A remittitur is the conditional grant of a new trial limited solely to damages. It is a device used to achieve the benefits of a new trial without having to spend time proceeding with a new trial.

The trial judge granted a new trial on the issue of damages alone unless Paul agreed to a reduction in the verdict from $75,000 to $25,000. This constitutes an order for a conditional new trial. The severity of Paul's injuries and the extent and nature of the damage evidence offered by Paul are unknown. These facts are necessary to determine whether the evidence reasonably supported the $75,000 award. Assuming the jury's damage award was excessive, the court's order must have been based on its good faith belief that the jury verdict was excessive.

Absent facts to the contrary, when Paul agreed to the reduction, even though under protest, this constituted his consent to accept the $25,000 award.

Some jurisdictions permit the plaintiff to consent to the remittitur without waiving his right to appeal the underlying conditional new trial ruling. An appeal is allowed, despite plaintiff's consent to remittitur, to ensure that the court did not abuse its discretion in conditionally requiring a second trial of the jury's damage award while preventing the added expense and waste of court time in a new trial.

However, other jurisdictions hold that, in order to preserve his right to appeal the underlying grant of the conditional new trial, a plaintiff would have to reject the remittitur and suffer the burden of a second trial on damages. If he consents to the remittitur of the jury award, the plaintiff waives his right to appeal.

Here, the plaintiff agreed under protest to a reduction of the jury's award. In those jurisdictions allowing an appeal in spite of assent to a remittitur, the plaintiff could properly maintain his cross-appeal. In the remaining jurisdictions, however, Paul's cross-appeal would be dismissed.

Thus, the remittitur may be valid.

CIVIL PROCEDURE QUESTION #5

PAULA v. MACCO

In 1976 Worker was injured by a defectively constructed machine while he was working in an industrial plant in State A. The machine had been manufactured by Macco, a State B corporation. While Worker was being treated for his injuries in Hospital in State A, Doctor, Worker's physician, prescribed medicine to which Worker was allergic. Worker's condition worsened gradually after that, but it was not clear whether his decline was due to the medicine or to his injuries.

Worker sued Hospital in a state court in State A for negligence. Hospital's defenses were (1) it was not responsible for the acts of Doctor, since he was an independent contractor, (2) Doctor had not been negligent, and (3) Worker's present condition was caused by his injury and not by the medicine. The trial court, sitting without a jury, found that Doctor had not acted negligently and that Doctor was not an agent of Hospital. The court made no finding on the cause of Worker's worsened condition. Judgment was entered for Hospital. No appeal was taken.

In 1978 Worker died and Worker's widow, Paula, who had lived in State A for five years, returned to her original home in State C. As executrix of her husband's estate duly qualified in State C, she filed suit in a state court in State C against Macco for the injuries to and the death of her husband. She also filed suit against Doctor in a state court in State A for the damages she sustained as a result of the death of her husband.

Macco makes sales in forty states and maintains an office in State C. During the past ten years, Macco has sold its products in State C. Its annual sales volume in that state is between $400,000 and $500,000. The machine that injured Worker was originally sold to a corporation in State A, which in turn had sold it to Worker's employer.

A statute in State C provides: "The courts of this state exercise jurisdiction over persons to the full extent permitted by the Constitution of the United States." None of these suits is barred by a statute of limitations.

1. Assuming appropriate objection by Macco, may State C exercise personal jurisdiction over Macco in Paula's suit as executrix? Discuss.

2. What effect, if any, does the judgment in Worker's suit in State A have on:

    (a) Paula's action in State C against Macco;
    (b) Paula's action in State A against Doctor?

Discuss.

IRAC OUTLINE SHEET

(I)	(R)	(A)	(C)

EXAMPLE OF PROPER OUTLINE

PAULA (P) v. MACCO (M)

(1) STATE C's PERSONAL JURISDICTION OVER MACCO:

(I)	(R)	(A)	(C)
PERSONAL JURISDICTION Long Arm Statute	Power To Bind Defendant Personally Legislative Act Non-Resident Defendant	P filed suit in State C court against M State C long arm statute permits jurisdiction over persons to the extent permitted by the U.S. Constitution M, a State B corporation	Valid Long Arm
DOES THE TRANSACTION FALL WITHIN STATUTE?	Tortious Act Must Occur In Forum Conservative-Where Harm Occurred Liberal-Wherever Harm Occurs	1976 Worker (W) injured by defective machine while working in State A plant Machine manufactured by M, a State B corp. W's widow P as executrix, duly qualified in State C filed suit in State C Machine originally sold to a corp. in State A which had it sold to W's employer	Transaction Within Liberal Jurisdiction
DUE PROCESS-MINIMUM CONTACTS	Minimum Contacts Purposeful Availment	M makes sales in 40 states Maintains office in State C during the past 10 years P returned to her original home in State C Machine sold to corp. in state A Injury occurred in State A Annual sales volume in State C of $400,000 to $500,000 for 10 years (foreseeability of injury?)	Minimum Contacts General Jurisdiction?
	Fair Play/Substantial Justice	P returned to her original home in State C Machine sold to corp. in state A Injury occurred in State A	
SERVICE OF PROCESS	Procedural Due Process Notice/Opportunity To Be Heard	No facts ?	Service Assumed Jurisdiction Present

(2) EFFECT OF THE JUDGMENT IN WORKER'S SUIT IN STATE A ON:

(a) P v. MACCO STATE C

(I)	(R)	(A)	(C)
RES JUDICATA	Valid Final Judgment On The Merits	State A judgment entered for H Judgment entered after court trial No appeal was taken	
	Precludes Reassertion Of Same Cause Of Action Same Parties Or Their Privies	W sued H in State A for negligence re: medical treatment P filed suit in state C against M for injuries to and the death of W P executrix of W's estate (M not same party or privy of H?)	No Res Judicata Effect
COLLATERAL ESTOPPEL	Precludes Relitigation As To Identical Issues In Second Lawsuit	1st suit W v. H Injuries from medicine/treatment 2nd suit P v. M Injuries from defective machine	
		P trying to assert (a) H/Doctor's nonliability (not agent)	Arguable Alternative Findings
	Actually Litigated/Necessarily Determined In Prior Suit	Issue #3 W's death caused by injury, not by medicine Court made no finding as to cause of W's worsened condition	
MUTUALITY RULE	C E May Only Be Asserted By & Against Parties/Privies (Split Of Jurisdictions)	M not a party to State A W v. H suit	Collateral Estoppel Effect ?
EXCEPTION: PARKLANE HOSIERY	A Nonparty Plaintiff May Use A Prior Judgment If Full And Fair Opportunity To Be Heard	P not named in original suit M not present at prior trial (opportunity to litigate causation?)	No Collateral Estoppel Effect

(b) P v. DOC (D) STATE A

(I)	(R)	(A)	(C)
RES JUDICATA	Valid Final Judgment On The Merits	Supra	
	Precludes Reassertion Of Same Cause Of Action	1st suit-negligence supra 2nd suit-wrongful death	No Res Judicata Effect
	Same Parties Or Their Privies	D was not party to 1st suit & not agent of H-independent contractor	

(I)	(R)	(A)	(C)
COLLATERAL ESTOPPEL	Precludes Relitigation As To Identical Issues In Second Lawsuit	1st suit-W v. H/H's negligence 2nd suit-P v. D/D's negligence	No Collateral Estoppel Alternative Finding
	Actually Litigated/Necessarily Determined In Prior Suit	P-executrix of W's estate Trial court found D not negligent/not agent of H	
MUTUALITY RULE	C E May Only Be Asserted By & Against Parties/Privies (Split Of Jurisdictions)	D not a party or privy to 1st suit	Collateral Estoppel Effect?
EXCEPTION: BERNHARD v. BANK OF AMERICA	A Nonparty Defendant May Use A Prior Judgment If Full & Fair Opportunity To Litigate The Issue	D not a party or privy to 1st suit P-executrix of W's estate In 1978 P sued D for negligence W sued H in 1976 (opportunity to litigate D's negligence?)	Collateral Estoppel Permitted

EXAMPLE OF IRAC CIVIL PROCEDURE ISSUE

(I) **Collateral Estoppel**

(R) Collateral estoppel precludes the (1) re-litigation of (2) an identical issue in a second lawsuit which was (3) actually litigated and necessarily determined in a prior suit.

(a) Paula v. Macco in State A: the issue of the doctor's negligence

(A) Paula will assert that the issue of (1) liability against the Hospital and the Doctor was determined in the State A suit and cannot be re-litigated. Since no liability was found against either defendant, by process of elimination, Macco must have been liable for negligence. The (2) issue of the doctor's negligent treatment of Worker is identical in both suits. The judge, in Worker v. Hospital, actually determined by his conclusive finding that the doctor had not acted negligently.

However, the judge (3) also actually determined that Doctor was not an agent of the Hospital. This presents a situation involving two independent, alternative findings by the judge, either one of which could explain why Hospital won. Courts are split in such situations. Some give collateral estoppel effect to both findings and, thus, the issue was necessarily determined. Others give collateral estoppel effect to neither finding (**Restatement 2d.**)

Further, Macco was not a party, nor or a privy of a party, in Worker v. Hospital. Macco did not have its day in court on the issue of the doctor's negligence. To allow Paula to invoke collateral estoppel would deny Macco of its Due Process rights.

(C) It appears doubtful that Paula could invoke the doctrine of collateral estoppel concerning the issue of Doctor's negligence.

SUGGESTED MODEL ANSWER

PAULA v. MACCO

1. MAY STATE C EXERCISE PERSONAL JURISDICTION OVER MACCO?

Personal Jurisdiction

Personal jurisdiction is the power of the court to render a judgment that will bind the defendant personally.

Since Paula filed suit in State C court against Macco pursuant to a long arm statute, she is attempting to invoke personal jurisdiction over Macco.

Long Arm Statute

A long arm statute is a state statute which authorizes a court of that state to exercise personal jurisdiction over non-residents by serving non-residents with process outside of the forum state.

The State C statute permits the State C court to exercise jurisdiction over persons to the extent permitted by the United States Constitution. Such precise language gives the State C court the power to bind Macco, a non-resident defendant by legislative statute. Therefore, through its long arm statute, State C may attempt to exercise personal jurisdiction over Macco, a non-resident State B Corporation.

Does the Transaction Fall Within the Long Arm Statute?

Long arm statutes will apply if the tortious act occurred in the forum. Liberal long arm statutes permit the exercise of jurisdiction irrespective of where the harm occurs. More conservative statutes allow jurisdiction only where the harm occurred within the forum.

Worker was injured in 1976 by a defective machine while working in an industrial plant in State A. The defective machine was manufactured by Macco in State B and sold to a corporation in State A. Macco's act of selling the defective machine to a corporation in State A that later sold it to Worker's employer would constitute a tortious act in State A.

Liberal jurisdictions would allow the suit against Macco in State C if all constitutional protections are met irrespective of the fact that the harm did not occur in State C, the forum state. Paula, as Worker's estate executrix duly qualified in State C, could validly file her suit there.

However, since Paula had failed to establish that the harm occurred within the forum state, a conservative jurisdiction would not allow suit against Macco in State C.

In liberal jurisdictions, the transaction falls within the long arm statute. Assuming the terms of the statute authorize the court to exercise personal jurisdiction over Macco, the exercise of personal jurisdiction over Macco must not violate Macco's rights under the Due Process Clause of the U.S. Constitution.

Due Process - Minimum Contacts

Under the case of **International Shoe**, the court may exercise jurisdiction over a defendant who is not present in the forum state only if that defendant has minimum contacts with the forum state such that the maintenance of the suit does not offend traditional notions of fair play and substantial justice.

Macco makes sales in forty states and maintains offices in State C. For 10 years, it has sold products in State C. Macco has had annual sales volume in State C of $400,000.00 to $500,000.00 for the past 10 years. This action demonstrates ongoing, deliberate conduct directed at State C.

Macco intends to serve the market in State C through the sale of its products demonstrated by the fact that it made $400,000 to $500,000 in annual sales to State C. As such, Macco has purposefully availed itself of the economic benefits and protections of State C law while engaging in its sales business. Such activity also subjects Macco to the burdens associated with doing business in that forum. Thus, Macco has sufficient contacts in that state to allow State C to exercise its jurisdiction over it.

The machine that injured Worker was sold to a corporation in State A where Worker was injured. Macco will contend that the foreseeability of injury was in State A, not in State C. Paula's claim does not directly arise out of those sales. Her claim arises directly out of Macco's sale of the machine in question to a corporation in State A which then sold the machine to Worker's employer. Therefore, Macco will contend that it should not reasonably expect to be sued by Paula in a court in State C on a claim arising out of the marketing of a machine to State A. Thus, the court in State C cannot exercise specific jurisdiction over Macco.

However, Paula will counter that Macco has done a large amount of business in State C over a period of 10 years. Presumably, its products include the type of machine that allegedly injured Worker. It has deliberately reached into State C by intentionally serving the market there. Although Paula's claim does not directly arise out of Macco's deliberate contacts with State C, Paula's claim does sufficiently relate to those contacts so that Macco should not reasonably be surprised at having to defend itself against Paula's suit in a State C court. Therefore, the threshold requirement of purposeful availment is satisfied.

As an alternative argument, Paula may try to persuade the court that Macco's contacts with State C are not only continuous and systematic but are also so substantial and of such a nature as to allow the court to assert general jurisdiction over Macco. General jurisdiction is a type of personal jurisdiction where the claim does not relate to the activities between the defendant and the forum state. $400,000 to $500,000 worth of sales annually for 10 years is fairly continuous and systematic. Macco maintains an office in State C. The potential for severe injuries created by the industrial machinery it sells there is predictable. Macco's close business ties to State C are so strong that it should reasonably expect to be sued in State C where its products are sold. Macco appears to have sufficient minimum contacts in State C.

At the time she filed suit in State C, Paula had returned to her original home in State C. State C has an interest in affording its citizens redress in its own courts. Paula, now the widow of a former factory worker, may not have the funds to sue long distance in State A. Macco presumably can better afford the cost of litigating long distance than Paula.

Macco will argue that Worker's death was caused by Worker's own negligence or by the negligence of the doctor that treated Worker in the hospital in State A. Thus, much of the evidence needed by Macco to support its defenses is located in State A, beyond the subpoena power of the court in State C. Macco would, therefore, argue that it would be fundamentally unfair to require it to defend itself in State C.

However, products liability disputes between manufacturers and consumers are always foreseeable. Macco should have reasonably expected to be sued in State C if a dispute arose concerning injuries related to machinery manufactured by Macco. State C is a fair and convenient forum in which to litigate Paula's claim.

Macco's contact in State C constitutes sufficient minimum contacts such that the maintenance of the suit in that jurisdiction does not offend traditional notions of fair play and substantial justice for purposes of litigation fairness.

Service of Process

The defendant must receive service of process allowing notice reasonably calculated to apprise it of the pendency of the action and an opportunity to be heard sufficient to satisfy the requirements of constitutional procedural due process (**Mullane.**)

There are no facts to indicate whether Macco was properly served. Such service is necessary to give Macco notice and an opportunity to be heard so that State C may exercise personal jurisdiction over the defendant.

Valid service of process must be assumed. Therefore, State C may exercise personal jurisdiction over Macco.

2. EFFECT OF THE JUDGMENT IN WORKER'S SUIT IN STATE A ON:

(A) PAULA v. MACCO IN STATE C

Res Judicata

A valid final judgment on the merits precludes a reassertion of the same cause of action in a subsequent action between the same parties or their privies.

After a court trial, State A judgment was entered for hospital in the case of Worker v. Hospital. Since no appeal was taken, the judgment as to the Hospital's liability is a valid judgment final on the merits.

The State A action was a suit in negligence for injuries from the medicine and treatment Worker received while in the Hospital. The State C suit is presumably in products liability for injuries Worker received from the defective machine. Assuming State A's res judicata law adopts the "same transaction" test, the claims asserted in the two suits arise out of different transactions (negligent medical treatment by a doctor vs. defective machine). Alternatively applying the "wrongs" test, the two suits involve different wrongful conduct (poor medical treatment vs. defect design and/or manufacture of the machine). Alternatively applying the "same evidence" test, the evidence relevant to each claim would be very different and, under the "rights" test, Worker sued on his right arising under malpractice law while Paula sued on a right arising under products liability law. Therefore, the causes of action are not the same.

Paula is the executrix of Worker's estate. She is deemed to have stepped into the shoes of the deceased and may be deemed to be a privy of her husband, Worker. If the wrongful death law in State C views Paula's claim as derivative of her husband's personal injury claim (and the facts state that Paula sued, in part, for the injuries to her husband), Paula will be deemed in privity with Worker. However, if State C tort law views wrongful death as the independent claim of the estate for injury to the surviving relatives like Paula, she may not be deemed a privy.

However, Macco was not a party to the State A suit. Hospital was the only defendant. Macco has no association with Hospital and is not a privy of or a party to that suit. For this reason alone, Macco cannot invoke res judicata to preclude Paula from asserting her claim against Macco.

The doctrine of res judicata is not applicable.

Collateral Estoppel

Collateral estoppel precludes the re-litigation of an identical issue in a second lawsuit which was actually litigated and necessarily determined in a prior suit.

(a) Paula v. Macco in State A: the issue of the doctor's negligence

Paula will assert that the issue of liability against the Hospital and the Doctor was determined in the State A suit and cannot be re-litigated. Since no liability was found against either defendant, by process of elimination, Macco must have been liable for negligence. The issue of the doctor's negligent treatment of Worker is identical in both suits. The judge, in Worker v. Hospital, actually determined by his conclusive finding that the doctor had not acted negligently.

However, the judge also actually determined that Doctor was not an agent of the Hospital. This presents a situation involving two independent, alternative findings by the judge, either one of which could explain why Hospital won. Courts are split in such situations. Some give collateral estoppel effect to both findings and, thus, the issue was necessarily determined. Others give collateral estoppel effect to neither finding (**Restatement 2d.**)
Further, Macco was not a party, nor or a privy of a party, in Worker v. Hospital. Macco did not have its day in court on the issue of the doctor's negligence. To allow Paula to invoke collateral estoppel would deny Macco of its Due Process rights.

It appears doubtful that Paula could invoke the doctrine of collateral estoppel concerning the issue of Doctor's negligence.

(b) Paula v. Macco in State C: the issue of the cause of Worker's injury

One of the affirmative defenses pled by Hospital in the State A suit was that Worker's death was caused by his injury and not by the medicine. This is the same issue being tried in the State C suit. Thus, the first judgment may be involved as to these identical issues.

However, State A court made no finding as to the cause of Worker's worsened condition. These essential facts are necessary to the determination of the causation issue. Therefore, the essential causation facts were never actually litigated and necessarily determined in the prior State A action.

It appears doubtful that Paula could invoke the doctrine of collateral estoppel concerning the issue of causation.

Mutuality Rule

If the doctrine of collateral estoppel is found applicable, the mutuality rule, which is the general rule, holds that it may only be asserted by and against parties and privies to the prior lawsuit. In a majority of jurisdictions, a nonparty may use a prior judgment to obtain relief (**Bernhard v. Bank of America.**)

Under the general rule, Paula could not assert the doctrine because she was not a party to the State A suit as discussed under Res Judicata supra.

However, in a majority of jurisdictions, Paula may be able to assert collateral estoppel in her favor.

Offensive Use - Sword

The **Parklane Hosiery** case permits a nonparty to use a prior judgment as a plaintiff to obtain relief against a defendant to the prior action.

Paula was not named in the prior Worker v. Hospital suit. Thus, she was a nonparty. Now, as a plaintiff in the State C suit, she is attempting to use the State A judgment for Hospital as a means of obtaining relief against Macco. Paula may invoke collateral estoppel offensively if the court determines, in its discretion, that it is fair to the Macco.

However, Macco will assert that it did not have its "day in court" guaranteed by the Due Process clause. Macco was not a defendant party in the State A suit and it never had a full and fair opportunity to litigate the issue of causation.

Therefore, Paula will be prevented from asserting the doctrine of collateral estoppel as a sword against Macco.

(B) PAULA v. DOCTOR IN STATE A

Res Judicata

Defined supra.

As established above, Worker's suit against Hospital was a valid final judgment on the merits as to the Doctor's independent contractor status and lack of negligence.

Doctor will contend that the first suit, Worker v. Hospital, was a negligence action and the second suit brought by Paula was for damages she sustained as a result of Worker's wrongful death. Since a wrongful death action sounds in negligence, the causes of action were the same. Paula's suit in State C is precluded because it is a reassertion of the same cause of action in the subsequent action.

However, Doctor was not a party to the first suit. Since he was found not to have been the agent of the Hospital due to his status as an independent contractor, he was not a privy to the action.

Doctor is not entitled to assert the doctrine of the res judicata.

Collateral Estoppel

Defined supra.

Doctor will argue that the first lawsuit brought by Worker against Hospital was for the Hospital's negligence. In the second suit, Paula is alleging the negligence of Doctor. Thus, he will contend that the claims are different.

Further, the trial court's finding that Doctor was not negligent on the issue of liability in the Worker suit should be invoked in the present suit.

As previously established, the issue of Doctor's negligence was the identical issue in both Worker v. Hospital and Paula v. Doctor. In Worker v. Hospital, the court found that Doctor was not negligent. That issue was actually litigated. However, the court also found that Doctor was not an agent of Hospital. Since that finding, standing alone, would require the court to find for Hospital, the court has made two independent, alternative findings. As discussed supra, jurisdictions are split on whether to give both or neither findings collateral estoppel effect.

In the first case there was a court trial and the court made a ruling concerning Doctor's treatment and lack of negligence. Thus, the essential facts regarding the issue were actually litigated and necessarily determined in the prior suit.

There is an issue whether Paula was in privity with Worker in his suit against Hospital. Paula has a plausible argument that the Due Process clause prevents Paula from being bound by the judgment in Worker v. Hospital because she was neither a party to, nor in privity with a party to, Worker v. Hospital.

The facts state that Paula brought suit against Macco in State C in her capacity as executrix and sued for the injuries to and the death of her husband. By contrast, the facts do not state that Paula brought suit against Doctor in her capacity as executrix and, in fact, state that she sued for damages that she (not her deceased husband) sustained as a result of the death of her husband. This different phraseology supports a reasonable inference that Paula is asserting an independent claim for her own damages rather than enforcing her husband's personal injury rights which passed to his estate upon his death

It appears that the doctrine of collateral estoppel is applicable.

Mutuality Rule

Defined supra.

Since the Doctor was not a party or privy to the earlier suit (supra), pursuant to the general rule, he would not be entitled to assert the doctrine of collateral estoppel. However, under the **Bernhard** rule, Doctor may be able to assert the doctrine in his favor.

Defensive Use - Shield

A nonparty may use a prior judgment as a defense against a party or privy with a party in the first suit if there was a full and fair opportunity to litigate the issue.

As a nonparty to the Worker v. Hospital suit, Doctor may use the already litigated issue of his lack of negligence as a defense to Paula's suit in State C.

Paula will rebut that she was not a party to the first suit. She is suing Doctor for her injuries, not Worker's. However, when she became the executrix of Worker's estate in 1978 and then sued for his injuries, she stepped into his shoes and would be considered a party. Thus, Paula was Worker's privy for the purposes of collateral estoppel.

In those jurisdictions that adopt the approach in **Bernard v. Bank of America**, mutuality does not automatically prevent a nonparty from using collateral estoppel as long as the opposing party had a full and fair opportunity to litigate the issue. The suits seem to be identical regarding the negligence of Doctor. A final judgment on the merits was entered. Worker had a full and fair opportunity to be heard at the first trial in 1976. There is no indication that Paula is in any better position to more fully litigate this issue than Worker. It appears Doctor has the stronger argument.

Therefore, the Doctor will be able to use the doctrine as a shield against Paula's suit.

SECTION VI

REAL PROPERTY

REAL PROPERTY

LEARN TO WRITE . . . THE RIGHT WAY®

REAL PROPERTY QUESTION #1

CITY v. GEORGE'S EXECUTORS

On June 1, 1973, in accordance with a written contract of sale, George deeded some land to City. On the land was a small open bandstand used for summer concerts. The deed contained this language: "To have and to hold so long as City uses the land for park purposes, and should City at any time stop using said land for park purposes, said land shall revert to George, his heirs and assigns forever."

The deed was placed in escrow with Local Loan on the oral understanding that City would deposit the purchase price within 60 days after the date of the deed. Before the deposit was made, the bandstand was destroyed by a fire of unknown origin. City deposited the purchase price in time, but contended that it was entitled to a deduction because of the fire loss. George disagreed, but authorized delivery of the deed and consented not to withdraw the money until they could negotiate the matter.

City took the deed and recorded it at once, but, because of the loss of the bandstand, began using the land for storage of City street department trucks. George immediately wrote to City objecting to the use of the land and advising City that he would instruct Local Loan to return the purchase price to City if City would immediately give up possession of the land and reconvey it to George. Three days later, before City had taken any further action, George died.

City then caused the execution and recordation of a deed of the land to George, removed all of the trucks from the land and has requested George's executor to instruct Local Loan to release the escrow funds to City.

George's executor wants to know whether he should comply with City's request and whether City would have a valid claim to either the land or the funds if he did not. What should he be advised?

Discuss.

IRAC OUTLINE SHEET

(I)	(R)	(A)	(C)

EXAMPLE OF PROPER IRAC OUTLINE

CITY (C) v. GEORGE'S (G) EXECUTORS

A. ESTATES CREATED BY DEED

(I)	(R)	(A)	(C)
FEE SIMPLE DEFEASIBLE	Estate Capable Of Indefinite Duration	6/1/73 in accordance with a written contract of sale, G deeded some land to C Deed contained language "to have and to hold so long as C uses land for park purposes"	Valid Fee Simple Defeasible
	Terminable On Happening Of Event	Should C at any time stop using land for park purposes, said land shall revert to G	
TYPE-FEE SIMPLE DETERMINABLE	Automatic End With Some Event	So long as C uses for park purposes	Valid Fee Simple Defeasible
	Grantor Maintains Possibility Of Reverter	Should C at any time stop using land for park purposes, said land shall revert to G	

B. DEED IN ESCROW

(I)	(R)	(A)	(C)
COMMERCIAL ESCROW	Irrevocable Delivery Deed	Deed placed in escrow	Valid Commercial Escrow
	Proper Selected Agent	Local Loan	
	Written Agreement	Oral understanding that C would deposit purchase price within 60 days after date of deed Written contract for sale	

C. BANDSTAND DESTRUCTION

(I)	(R)	(A)	(C)
EQUITABLE CONVERSION	Valid Executory Land Sales Contract	6/1/73 written contract of sale deeded land Deed placed in escrow	Equitable Conversion
	Buyer Holds Equitable Title	C deposited purchase price in time	
	Seller Holds Legal Title	G	
RISK OF LOSS	Property Destroyed During Executory Stage Majority Rule-Loss on Buyer Minority Rule-Loss on Seller CA Statute-Loss On Seller Absent Buyer Taking Title/Possession	Before deposit made bandstand destroyed by fire of unknown origin C deposited purchase price in time/contended was entitled to deduction because of fire loss/G disagreed	Split of Jurisdiction

D. DELIVERY FROM ESCROW

(I)	(R)	(A)	(C)
COMMERCIAL ESCROW	Irrevocable Delivery	G authorized delivery of deed/consented not to withdraw S until they could negotiate matter	Valid Commercial Escrow
	Proper Selected Agent	Local Loan	
	Written Agreement	C took deed/recorded it at once	

(I)	(R)	(A)	(C)
E. TERMINATION OF FEE SIMPLE DETERMINABLE	Automatic End With Some Event	So long as C used for park purposes/C began using land for storage of C street dept. trucks	City Has No Valid Interest
	Grantor Maintains Possibility Of A Reverter	Should C at any time stop using for park purposes, land shall revert to G immediately wrote to C objecting to use	

EXAMPLE OF IRAC REAL PROPERTY ISSUE

(I) **Risk Of Loss**

(R) When property is damaged or destroyed while a while a land sales contract is in its executory stage, (1) the majority of courts put the risk of loss on the buyer. (2) A minority of courts put the risk of loss on the seller. (3) California, by statute, places the risk on the seller absent the buyer taking title or possession.

(A) Before City made its deposit into escrow, the bandstand on the property in question was destroyed by a fire of unknown origin. Afterwards, City did make its purchase price deposit in time but contended that it was entitled to a deduction in the purchase price because of the fire loss. George disagreed. Even though the sales contract was still in its executory stages at the time of the fire, (1) a majority of courts would place the risk of loss on the buyer, City, because it was the equitable owner under the doctrine of equitable conversion discussed supra. As a result, City would not be entitled to a deduction for the loss of the bandstand.

(2) In a minority of jurisdictions, the risk of loss would be placed on the seller, George. If City can show that the loss of the bandstand was substantial and the terms of contract show that the bandstand constituted an important part of the subject matter of the contract, City may demand specific performance with an abatement in the purchase price for the amount of the damage. However, absent facts to the contrary, it appears that the bandstand was incidental to the contract as City was willing to complete the sale despite the bandstand destruction.

(3) In California, by statute, the risk of loss passes to the seller, George, absent the City taking title or possession of the property. Since the City had done neither and George had not relinquished title or possession, he would bear the risk of loss in California jurisdictions.

(C) Therefore, under the majority rule the risk of loss is on City.

SUGGESTED MODEL ANSWER

CITY v. GEORGE'S EXECUTORS

Estates Created By Deed - Fee Simple Defeasible

A fee simple defeasible is an estate capable of an indefinite duration that can be terminated on the happening of some event.

On June 1, 1973, in accordance with a written contract of sale, George deeded some land to City "to have...so long as City uses the land for park purposes." Such language created an estate capable of an infinite duration as long as City used the land for the specified purpose.

The deed further stated "should City at any time stop using said land for park purposes, said land shall revert...." Violation of this land use restriction is the happening of an event that creates grounds for termination of the fee.

A fee simple defeasible was created.

Type - Fee Simple Determinable

A fee simple determinable is a fee estate so limited that it will automatically end when some specified event happens. The grantor maintains a future interest deemed a possibility of reverter.

When George inserted the language "so long as City uses for park purposes", those words created a limitation on the use of the land. Any other use constituted a specified event that would automatically act to end the duration of the fee estate.

George, the grantor, further inserted the language "should City stop using for park purposes, said land shall revert to George." As such, he maintained a future interest called a possibility of reverter which would cause the land to revert back to him, by operation of law, in the event that City did not comply with the limitation.

George created a fee simple determinable.

Deed In Escrow - Commercial Escrow

A commercial escrow occurs when a seller irrevocably delivers a deed naming the buyer as grantee to a proper selected escrow agent with written instructions to hand the deed to the grantee when and if, before a fixed date, the grantee fulfills certain conditions.

George placed the deed in escrow with Local Loan. Such a deposit would be considered an irrevocable delivery. Absent facts to the contrary, Local Loan was a proper selected escrow agent. The opening of escrow was on the oral understanding that City would deposit the purchase price within 60 days after the date of the deed. Such an oral instruction would be considered valid in the presence of the written contract of sale and thus would not violate the Statute of Frauds.

It appears that a valid commercial escrow was opened.

Bandstand Destruction

Equitable Conversion

During the period of escrow while a valid land sales contract is in its executory stages, the buyer holds equitable title to the land and the seller holds the bare legal title in trust for the buyer as security for the debt owed the seller.

On 6/1/73, George entered into a valid written land sales contract with City. He then placed the deed in escrow while the contract was still in its executory stage. City deposited the purchase price within the 60 days specified by George. City, the buyer, would hold title as the equitable title owner of the land. George, the seller, would hold the bare legal title to it as security until the close of escrow. Equity would regard the performance of the sales contract as done since that is what ought to have been done during the period of escrow. Either party could then demand specific performance.

The doctrine of equitable conversion may be invoked.

Risk Of Loss

When property is damaged or destroyed while a land sales contract is in its executory stage, the majority of courts put the risk of loss on the buyer. A minority of courts put the risk of loss on the seller. California, by statute, places the risk on the seller absent the buyer taking title or possession.

Before City made its deposit into escrow, the bandstand on the property in question was destroyed by a fire of unknown origin. Afterwards, City did make its purchase price deposit in time but contended that it was entitled to a deduction in the purchase price because of the fire loss. George disagreed. Even though the sales contract was still in its executory stages at the time of the fire, a majority of courts would place the risk of loss on the buyer, City, because it was the equitable owner under the doctrine of equitable conversion discussed supra. As a result, City would not be entitled to a deduction for the loss of the bandstand.

In a minority of jurisdictions, the risk of loss would be placed on the seller, George. If City can show that the loss of the bandstand was substantial and the terms of contract show that the bandstand constituted an important part of the subject matter of the contract, City may demand specific performance with an abatement in the purchase price for the amount of the damage. However, absent facts to the contrary, it appears that the bandstand was incidental to the contract as City was willing to complete the sale despite the bandstand destruction.

In California, by statute, the risk of loss passes to the seller, George, absent the City taking title or possession of the property. Since the City had done neither and George had not relinquished title or possession, he would bear the risk of loss in California jurisdictions.

Therefore, under the majority rule the risk of loss is on City.

Delivery From Escrow - Commercial Escrow

Defined supra.

George authorized Local Loan, the proper selected agent, to deliver the deed from escrow to City after City had deposited its purchase price. The fact that George consented not to withdraw the money until he and City could negotiate the matter of the bandstand destruction does not effect the irrevocability of the delivery. When City took the deed and recorded it at once, City's right to the land based on these written documents of agreement was perfected.

A valid delivery from a commercial escrow was executed.

Termination Of Fee Simple Determinable

Defined supra.

When City began using the land for storage of City street department trucks in violation of the limitation to use it for park purposes only, such an event would act to automatically end the duration for which its fee had been granted.

George immediately wrote to City objecting to the use. This action demonstrated his intent to enforce the original terms of the conveyance. However, because a fee simple determinable was created, there is no need for George to do anything to demonstrate his intent.

Since City's use of the land for storage trucks is found to be outside that permitted under the deed, title to the property automatically reverts back to George. Upon his death, the executor took over administration of the estate. George's executor does not have to comply with City's request. City has no valid claim to the land or to the funds.

REAL PROPERTY QUESTION #2

LANDLORD v. TENANT

Landlord rented an apartment in his building to Tenant for one year beginning June 1, 1970. On June 1, Tenant was unable to move in because the apartment was still occupied by Billy, whose lease had expired May 31. Billy eventually moved out on June 30 and Tenant moved in on July 1. During July, a hailstorm caused two broken windowpanes in Tenant's apartment. Tenant demanded that Landlord replace the windowpanes. Landlord replied that Tenant had to do it. Rain coming in through the broken panes caused considerable damage to the wallpaper and floors.

The apartment directly above Tenant's was occupied by Charlie, a member of the famous rock group, "The Charles River". The daily rehearsals of his group interfered with Tenant's law studies and sleep so much that he complained repeatedly to Landlord. On July 15, three of Charlie's friends were arrested in his apartment and charged with possession of narcotics. On August 31, Tenant moved out without ever having paid any rent to Landlord.

What are Landlord's rights, if any, against Tenant? His liabilities? Discuss.

IRAC OUTLINE SHEET

(I)	(R)	(A)	(C)

EXAMPLE OF PROPER IRAC OUTLINE

LANDLORD (L) v. TENANT (T)

TYPE OF LEASEHOLD

(I)	(R)	(A)	(C)
TENANCY FOR YEARS	Non -Freehold Estate	L rented an apt. in his building to T	Tenancy For Years
	Beginning/Ending Dates	One year beginning June 1, 1970	
	Expires Without Notice	One year from June 1, 1970	
DELIVERY OF POSSESSION	C/L Minority - Duty To Deliver Legal Possession	T rented apt. beginning June 1, 1970	Split of Jurisdictions
	M/L Majority - Must Deliver Actual And Legal Right To Possession	On June 1, T unable to move in because the apt. was still occupied by B whose lease had expired May 31/B eventually moved out on June 30 and T moved in on July 1 (L liable to T for damages?)	
HAILSTORM DAMAGE			
DUTY TO REPAIR	C/L - No Duty To Repair M/L - Duty to Keep Premises Habitable	During July a hailstorm caused two broken windowpanes in T's apt. T demanded that L replace the windowpanes/L replied that T had to do it/rain coming in through broken panes caused considerable damage to wallpaper and floors T moved out August 31 supra	Split of Jurisdictions
DUTY TO MAINTAIN HABITABLE PREMISES	C/L - No Duty To Keep Habitable M/L - Affirmative Duty To Keep Habitable	July hailstorm caused two broken windowpanes supra Rain coming in through the broken panes caused considerable damage to wallpaper and floors T moved out on August 31 without ever having paid any rent to L	Split of Jurisdictions
EFFECT OF REHEARSALS			
COVENANT OF QUIET USE/ENJOYMENT	Right Of Use & Enjoyment Without Substantial Interference By Landlord	The apt. directly above T's was occupied by C, a member of the rock group "TCR"/the daily rehearsals of his group interfered with T's law studies and sleep so much that he complained repeatedly to L	Breach Of Covenant
CONSTRUCTIVE EVICTION	Substantial Interference Use/Enjoyment of Tenant Landlord At Fault T Must Vacate	Daily rehearsals - supra T repeatedly complained to L On August 31, T moved out without ever having paid any rent to L	Constructive Eviction
DUTY TO MAINTAIN HABITABLE PREMISES	C/L - No Duty To Keep Habitable M/L - Affirmative Duty To Keep Habitable	Rehearsals interfered with law studies and sleep supra/repeated complaints supra	Split Of Jurisdictions
NARCOTICS ARREST			
DUTY TO MAINTAIN HABITABLE PREMISES	C/L - No Duty To Keep Habitable M/L - Affirmative Duty To Keep Habitable	On July 15, 3 of C's friends were arrested in his apt. and charged with possession of narcotics On August 31, T moved out supra	No Breach
CONSTRUCTIVE EVICTION	Substantial Interference Use/Enjoyment Of Tenant Landlord At Fault Tenant Must Vacate	On July 15, 3 of C's friends arrested supra ∅, On August 31, T moved out	No Constructive Eviction
ABANDONMENT	T Unjustly Abandons Premises L's Options: 1) Let Premises Remain Vacant-Sue For Rent 2) Repossess & Relet 3) Accept Abandonment 4) Sue For Breach Of Contract	On August 31, T moved out without ever having paid any rent to L	Arguable

EXAMPLE OF IRAC REAL PROPERTY ISSUE

(I) **Constructive Eviction**

(R) Constructive eviction permits a tenant to terminate the lease and be excused from rental obligation if there is (1) substantial interference with tenant's use and enjoyment of the premises, (2) the landlord is at fault, and (3) the tenant vacates the premises.

(A) Tenant will argue that the daily rehearsals by The Charles River rock group in the apartment directly above his created such a disturbance that Tenant was unable to study his law or sleep. This rock band noise should be regarded as fundamentally incompatible with the residential purposes for which Tenant rented the apartment.

Therefore, the daily rehearsals would constitute a (1) substantial interference with the use and enjoyment of the premises.

Further, the extent of the interference to Tenant's law studies and sleep was so substantial that he complained repeatedly to Landlord. These complaints over the protracted two months of Tenant's period of tenancy gave Landlord ample notice of the Charlie Rivers objectionable conduct. Since Landlord had a duty to abate the noise created by Charlie and the legal ability to do so, (2) he was at fault when he failed to remedy the situation during that period of time.

(C) Therefore, (3) Tenant was justified in vacating the premises on August 31. His action would serve to terminate the lease and he would be excused from further rent obligation.

SUGGESTED MODEL ANSWER

LANDLORD v. TENANT

Type of Leasehold - Tenancy for Years

A tenancy for years is a non-freehold estate with a fixed beginning and an automatic ending date wherein the tenancy expires without notice.

When Landlord rented an apartment in his building to Tenant, he created a non-freehold estate in Tenant. The lease was for a period of one year beginning June 1, 1970. That date created a fixed beginning and automatic ending date. Tenant's tenancy would expire without the necessity that either party give notice of the expiration of the lease period.

A tenancy for years was created.

Duty to Deliver Possession

Under common law and a minority of jurisdictions, a landlord has a duty only to deliver legal possession. Under the majority rule, a landlord has the duty to deliver both actual and the legal right to possession to the tenant at the beginning of the tenancy.

Landlord will contend that under both common law and a minority of jurisdictions, Tenant was given legal right to possession by virtue of the June 1, 1970 rental date. It was up to Tenant to take possession of the apartment. Since Billy was a holdover tenant, Landlord is not liable to Tenant for Billy's conduct. Tenant should have exercised his right to evict Billy rather than waiting for him to eventually move out on June 1, thirty days after his rental expiration date.

However, under the majority rule, a Landlord has a duty to deliver both actual as well as the legal right to possession to Tenant on June 1, 1970. Tenant will assert that by allowing Billy to occupy Tenant's apartment until June 30, despite the expiration of his lease, Landlord failed to exercise his duty to deliver actual and legal possession at the beginning of Tenant's period of tenancy.

Thus, Landlord's failure to evict Billy within a reasonable time constituted a breach of his duty to deliver possession.

Landlord has no right to demand rent from Tenant during the month in which he was kept out of possession. Further, Tenant may have a right to damages from the Landlord if he incurred any losses during the one month period he was kept out of actual possession.

The type of jurisdiction will determine the extent of the Landlord's liability.

Hailstorm Damage

Duty to Repair

At common law, a landlord had no duty to repair the premises after a tenant had gone into possession. Modernly, a covenant of habitability is implied in residential leases imposing upon a landlord the duty to repair and maintain a habitable premises for the duration of the tenancy.

During July, a hailstorm caused two broken windowpanes in Tenant's apartment. Landlord will assert that since Tenant had gone into actual possession at that time (supra), under common law, Landlord had no duty to repair the windowpanes. Further, Landlord will assert that it was Tenant's obligation to make ordinary repairs to maintain the premises. Repair of the panes fell within the purview of Tenant's own responsibility. By permitting rain to come in through the broken panes causing considerable damage to the wallpaper and floor, Tenant committed permissive waste and is liable to the Landlord for damages.

However, Tenant will assert that the majority of jurisdictions do not require a tenant to make substantial repairs to the premises, especially in an instance where it was an act of God that was responsible for the pane damage. Further, a majority of jurisdictions place the burden of repair on the landlord through an implied covenant of habitability.

The damage to the panes, wallpaper and floor created an unhealthful and unsafe condition in the apartment making it unsuitable for the residential use contemplated by both parties. As such, Tenant will argue that it was unfit for human habitation.

By Landlord's failure to repair the condition, despite timely notice of the condition by way of Tenant's demands for him to do so, Landlord breached his duty to the Tenant justifying Tenant's action of moving out on August 31.

Since Tenant's duty to pay rent is dependent upon Landlord's performance of his duties under the implied warranty of habitability, he would also be justified in refusing to pay any rent.

However, if the damage to his apartment is not found to have rendered it uninhabitable, Tenant will not be justified in moving or withholding rent. Further, given the fact that repairing two panes of glass is relatively minor when compared to the eventual damage caused by the Tenant's permissive waste, Tenant should have mitigated his damages by repairing the panes before the premises became uninhabitable.

Landlord may seek rent for the months Tenant was in possession of the apartment in addition to the rent owed for the remainder of the tenancy period.

The type of jurisdiction will determine the extent of the Landlord's liability.

Duty to Maintain Habitable Premises

At common law, a landlord had no duty to maintain a premises in habitable condition. Modernly, a majority of jurisdictions have implied a continuing covenant of habitability on landlord's part in leases of residential dwellings.

Landlord will rely on the common law rule in arguing that he had no duty to maintain the integrity of the windowpanes in the condition they were in prior to the hailstorm. His argument will extend to the wallpaper and floor as well. These conditions are aesthetic in nature only and have no impact on habitability.

However modernly, conditions that occur during the life of the tenancy requiring maintenance through no fault of the tenant falls within the purview of Landlord's implied covenant of habitability. The hailstorm and subsequent rain damage to the wallpaper and floors were not caused through any fault on Tenant's part but rather an act of God. Although Tenant should probably bear some responsibility for his failure to mitigate the relatively minor window pane damage, the court will likely find that Landlord had an obligation to correct and maintain the premises in its original condition of habitability.

Landlord has breached his duty to maintain a habitable premises. In the majority of jurisdictions, Landlord will not be able to recover any rent from Tenant during this period.

Effect of Rehearsals

Covenant of Quiet Use and Enjoyment

A tenant has a right of quiet use and enjoyment of the premises without substantial interference by the landlord.

The apartment directly above Tenant's was occupied by Charlie, a member of the famous rock group, The Charles River. Tenant will assert that the rock group's daily rehearsals interfered with his law studies and sleep to the point that he was unable to use and enjoy the premises for residential purposes. His repeated complaints to Landlord went unanswered. Landlord's failure to take affirmative steps to eliminate the noise from the rehearsals constituted a breach of Landlord's implied covenant to provide quiet use and enjoyment of the premises.

Landlord will counter that while the rehearsals may have constituted a substantial interference with Tenant's use and enjoyment of his apartment, they were not caused by him but rather by Charlie, another tenant.

However, Tenant would successfully argue that by permitting one tenant to substantially interfere with another's enjoyment, the Landlord is himself responsible for that interference.

Therefore, Landlord is in breach of the implied covenant of quiet use and enjoyment.

Constructive Eviction

Constructive eviction permits a tenant to terminate the lease and be excused from rental obligation if there is substantial interference with tenant's use and enjoyment of the premises, the landlord is at fault, and the tenant vacates the premises.

Tenant will argue that the daily rehearsals by The Charlie River rock group in the apartment directly above his created such a disturbance that Tenant was unable to study his law or sleep. This rock band noise should be regarded as fundamentally incompatible with the residential purposes for which Tenant rented the apartment.

Therefore, the daily rehearsals would constitute a substantial interference with the use and enjoyment of the premises.

Further, the extent of the interference to Tenant's law studies and sleep was so substantial that he complained repeatedly to Landlord. These complaints over the protracted two months of Tenant's period of tenancy gave Landlord ample notice of the Charlie Rivers objectionable conduct. Since Landlord had a duty to abate the noise created by Charlie and the legal ability to do so, he was at fault when he failed to remedy the situation during that period of time.

Therefore, Tenant was justified in vacating the premises on August 31. His action would serve to terminate the lease and he would be excused from further rent obligation.

Duty to Maintain Habitable Premises

Defined supra.

Landlord will assert that under common law, even though the daily rock band rehearsals in the apartment directly above Tenant's may have interfered with Tenant's law studies and sleep, if Tenant inspected the premises prior to taking possession, he would have known about these daily rehearsals. His failure to do so would not create a duty on Landlord's part to intervene so that Tenant's apartment would be fit for residential living. Tenant would have to take the apartment as is, daily rehearsals included.

However, if the rehearsals were going on before Tenant took possession, modern jurisdictions would not consider such daily disturbances suitable to residential uses. Since the condition existed at the inception of Tenant's tenancy, Landlord would have a duty to correct the problem. Failure to do so would put Landlord in breach of his duty to maintain the implied covenant of habitability.

Therefore, Tenant would have a defense to an action by Landlord for nonpayment of rent.

Narcotics Arrest

Duty to Maintain Habitable Premises

Defined supra.

On July 15, three of Charlie's friends were arrested in Charlie's apartment and charged with possession of narcotics. Tenant will assert that such illegal activity in the apartment located directly above his created danger to those living in the apartment complex making it uninhabitable for residential purposes.

However, there are no facts to indicate that Landlord was either aware of the drug use in Charlie's apartment or that he had been notified of the situation prior to the arrest. Absent a showing that Landlord knew or was on notice of the narcotics use and failed to fulfill an obligation to remedy the situation, no liability will be imposed either under common or modern law jurisdictions. For that reason, Tenant was not justified in moving out on August 31.

Landlord has not breached his duty to maintain a habitable premises with respect to the narcotics arrest.

Constructive Eviction

Defined supra.

Tenant will contend that the narcotics arrests in Charlie's apartment created the type of illegal social climate that substantially interfered with Tenant's use and enjoyment of his own apartment. Tenant had contemplated only residential activities on the premises when he entered into the lease. Narcotics use by other tenants directly above his apartment fell outside this contemplated use.

However, absent a showing of fault on the part of Landlord, it does not appear that Landlord was aware of or had a duty to remedy the situation. No health or safety violations were directed at Tenant as a result of the arrests. As such, Tenant was not justified as using this as a basis to vacate the apartment or to refuse to pay rent.

The narcotics arrests will not constitute grounds for constructive eviction.

Abandonment

If a tenant unjustifiably abandons the premises, the landlord may allow the premises to remain vacant and sue the tenant as rent comes due, repossess and relet the premises, accept tenant's abandonment, or sue for breach of contract.

If Tenant is found to have unjustifiably abandoned the premises, Landlord has four options: He may allow the apartment to remain vacant and sue Tenant as the monthly rent becomes due, he may repossess and relet the apartment to another tenant, accept Tenant's abandonment which is equivalent to a surrender, or sue Tenant for breach of contract under the original lease.

If, however, any of the breaches previously discussed give Tenant justification for abandoning the premises, Landlord will have no rights against Tenant.

The jurisdiction where this matter is heard will determine whether Tenant was justified in moving from the premises on August 31 without paying any rent.

REAL PROPERTY QUESTION #3

WHO OWNS GREENACRE?

In 1950 Owens purported to sell Greenacre to Able for $1,000 cash. Greenacre is a parcel of unimproved mountain land which is inaccessible by road during six months of each year due to snow. Owens gave Able a deed which granted Greenacre to Able in fee simple and contained all warranties of title. Able did not have a title examination made. Able immediately recorded his deed and obtained an unsecured loan from Bank, and used the funds to build a vacation cabin on the land. Unknown to Able, Owens' grandfather was the true and sole owner of Greenacre.

From 1950 to the present, Able has paid taxes on Greenacre and lived in the cabin for one month each summer. The cabin and land have otherwise been unoccupied. Bank placed a sign on the land at the time of construction which read: "Built with financing from Bank." The sign has remained in place, readily observable, ever since.

In 1973, Owens borrowed $5,000 from Charlie. In 1977 Owens' grandfather died, leaving Greenacre to Owens by will. In the winter of 1978 Charlie induced Owens to deed Greenacre in full satisfaction of the $5,000 debt, which was then past due. Charlie had no actual notice of Able's claim to Greenacre.

Title searches in the state are customarily made in the grantor-grantee indexes of the official record. The recording statute reads:

"Any unrecorded conveyance is deemed void as against a subsequent taker for value and without notice."

Who owns Greenacre? Discuss.

IRAC OUTLINE SHEET

(I)	(R)	(A)	(C)

EXAMPLE OF PROPER IRAC OUTLINE

WHO OWNS GREENACRE?

I. ABLE'S (A) RIGHTS TO GREENACRE (G)

(I)	(R)	(A)	(C)
RECORDING ACT-BFP	Subsequent Purchaser	1950 O purported to sell G to A O gave A deed/granted G to A in fee simple	A Not A BFP
	Valuable Consideration	$1,000	
	Without Notice	G is a parcel of unimproved mountain land (inquiry notice?) O gave A deed that granted G to A in fee simple contained all warranties of title A did not have a title examination made A immediately recorded his deed Unknown to A, O's grandfather was the true and sole owner of G (actual notice?) Title searches in the state are customarily made in the grantor-grantee indexes of official records (constructive notice?)	
ESTOPPEL BY DEED	Grantor Conveys Before Title Ownership	1950 0 purported to sell G/grandfather true owner supra	Jurisdictional Split
	Grantor Subsequently Acquires Title (Operation Of Law)	Deed contained all warranties of title 1977 O's grandfather died leaving G to O by will/1978 Charlie induced O to deed G to him	
WARRANTIES OF TITLE	General Warranty Deed	1950 O gave A a deed which granted G to A in fee simple & contained all warranties of title	No Rights Under Present Warranties
	Contains Six Present/Future Covenants	1950 to present-(statute of limitations?)	
	Defect Arising Before/During Grantor Had Title	O did not have title to G in 1950 C induced O to deed G	Valid Rights Under Future Warranties
ADVERSE POSSESSION	Hostile	A immediately recorded his deed Obtained an unsecured loan from bank O's grandfather true sole owner	Valid Adverse Possession
	Open/Notorious	1950 to present, A paid taxes B placed sign on land at time of construction reading "Built with financing from B" Sign has remained in place, readily observable ever since G inaccessible by road during 6 months each year due to snow	
	Actual	A lived in cabin one month each summer	
	Continuous	1950 to present, A lived in cabin one month each summer	

II. CHARLIE'S (C) RIGHTS TO GREENACRE

(I)	(R)	(A)	(C)
RECORDING ACT-BFP	Subsequent Purchaser	1973 O borrowed $5,000 from C 1978 C induced O to deed 1973 O borrowed $5,000 from C/G deeded to C in full satisfaction of the $5,000 debt	Recording Statute Invalid
	Valuable Consideration	Debt was then past due (antecedent debt)	
	Without Notice	1950 O purported to sell G to A/A immediately recorded supra 1977 G left to O by will supra C had no actual knowledge of A's claim to G (constructive notice?) Inaccessible/built vacation cottage supra (inquiry?) Grantor-grantee index system supra (estoppel by deed supra) (adverse possession-operation of law) Any unrecorded conveyance deemed void against a subsequent taker for value and without notice	
PRIOR-IN-TIME RULE	First In Time-First In Right	O purported to sell to A in 1950 1977 G left to O by will 1978 C induced O to deed G in satisfaction of debt supra	A Prior-In-Time

EXAMPLE OF IRAC REAL PROPERTY ISSUE

(I) **Recording Act - Bona Fide Purchaser for Value**

(R) In a notice jurisdiction, (1) a subsequent purchaser giving (2) valuable consideration and (3) taking without notice of a prior interest qualifies as a bona fide purchaser who will be protected by the recording act.

(A) In 1950, Owens purported to sell Greenacre to Able. By virtue of the land sales agreement granting the property to Able in fee simple, (1) Able was a subsequent purchaser.

The $1,000.00 Able paid for Greenacre constituted (2) valuable consideration.

Able will assert that Owens gave him a deed which granted Greenacre to Able in fee simple. The deed contained all warranties of title. Unknown to him, Owens' grandfather was the true and sole owner. Thus, the delivery of an apparently valid, authentic deed together with his lack of knowledge concerning the true ownership, demonstrated that his purchase of Greenacre was (3) without actual notice of the grandfather's interest.

Greenacre is a parcel of unimproved mountain land. If Able had conducted a reasonable search of the property itself, he would not have been put on inquiry notice of the grandfather's interest.

However, Able did not have a title examination of the deed made before he purchased and then immediately recorded his deed. Title searches in that state were customarily made in the grantor/grantee indexes of the official records. If he had conducted the record search in the available official records designated for this purpose before he immediately recorded his own deed, Able would have discovered that Owens was not the true owner of Greenacre. If the grandfather's deed was recorded, this would have given him constructive notice of Owens' grandfather's true and sole ownership.

It is possible, however, that Able would not have discovered that Owens was not the true owner of Greenacre unless there was something on the record to be found in a title examination. There are no facts stating that the grandfather received the property by a deed or other recordable instrument, or that the instrument was actually recorded.

Assuming the grandfather's interest in Greenacre was on record and because this state's recording statute protects only subsequent takers without notice, Able would not qualify as a bona fide purchaser for value even though he did immediately record his deed in 1950.

(C) Therefore, Able would not be protected by the recording statute.

SUGGESTED MODEL ANSWER

I. ABLE'S RIGHT TO GREENACRE

Recording Act - Bona Fide Purchaser for Value

In a notice jurisdiction, a subsequent purchaser giving valuable consideration and taking without notice of a prior interest qualifies as a bona fide purchaser who will be protected by the recording act.

In 1950, Owens purported to sell Greenacre to Able. By virtue of the land sales agreement granting the property to Able in fee simple, Able was a subsequent purchaser.

The $1,000.00 Able paid for Greenacre constituted valuable consideration.

Able will assert that Owens gave him a deed which granted Greenacre to Able in fee simple. The deed contained all warranties of title. Unknown to him, Owens' grandfather was the true and sole owner. Thus, the delivery of an apparently valid, authentic deed together with his lack of knowledge concerning the true ownership, demonstrated that his purchase of Greenacre was without actual notice of the grandfather's interest.

Greenacre is a parcel of unimproved mountain land. If Able had conducted a reasonable search of the property itself, he would not have been put on inquiry notice of the grandfather's interest.

However, Able did not have a title examination of the deed made before he purchased and then immediately recorded his deed. Title searches in that state were customarily made in the grantor/grantee indexes of the official records. If he had conducted the record search in the available official records designated for this purpose before he immediately recorded his own deed, Able would have discovered that Owens was not the true owner of Greenacre. If the grandfather's deed was recorded, this would have given him constructive notice of Owens' grandfather's true and sole ownership.

It is possible, however, that Able would not have discovered that Owens was not the true owner of Greenacre unless there was something on the record to be found in a title examination. There are no facts stating that the grandfather received the property by a deed or other recordable instrument, or that the instrument was actually recorded.

Assuming the grandfather's interest in Greenacre was on record and because this state's recording statute protects only subsequent takers without notice, Able would not qualify as a bona fide purchaser for value even though he did immediately record his deed in 1950.

Therefore, Able would not be protected by the recording statute.

Estoppel by Deed

Under a minority of jurisdictions, where a grantor purports to convey an interest in property that he does not then own at that time but then subsequently acquires, the title passes to the grantee under the earlier deed by operation of law.

As previously stated, when Owens purported to sell Greenacre to Able in 1950, he did so despite the fact he did not then own title to the property. However, by giving Able a deed containing all warranties of title, he impliedly covenanted that when he obtained title from his grandfather, the true and sole owner, he would immediately convey it to Able.

When Owens' grandfather died in 1977 leaving Greenacre to Owens by will, Owens' subsequent acquisition of title inured to the benefit of Able. Therefore, in order to carry out the intent of the contracting parties and avoid unnecessary litigation, title to Greenacre passed to Able under the earlier deed. Able would be deemed the owner of the property by operation of law.

In a majority of jurisdictions, where there is a recorded deed from a grantor who has no title but who afterwards obtains title and then conveys to a bona fide purchaser, estoppel by deed will not apply against that bona fide purchaser.

Charlie induced Owens to deed Greenacre to him in 1978 after Owens had received Greenacre by will. Charlie will argue that as a subsequent bona fide purchaser, his rights arose subsequent to Able's rights under estoppel by deed. In this instance, Able's rights to Greenacre may be defeated. This application will be discussed under Charlie's rights to Greenacre.

Warranties of Title - General Warranty Deed

The extent of the seller's liability for a defect in title is governed by the covenants of title contained in the deed. A general warranty deed contains all six of the present and future covenants which warrants title against defects arising before as well as during the time the grantor had title.

When Owens purported to sell Greenacre to Able in 1950, he gave Able a deed which granted Greenacre to Able in fee simple and contained all warranties of title, i.e. a general warranty deed. This language guaranteed the enforceability of the present covenants of seisen, the right to convey and a right against encumbrances. Also, future covenants of quiet enjoyment, warranty against lawful claims and further assurances were included by the above-stated language. Thus, Able's deed warranted his title against any and all defects arising before as well as during the time Owens had title to Greenacre.

As previously established, Owens did not, in fact, have title to Greenacre in 1950. Therefore, Owens breached the covenant of seisin, and the right to convey at the moment he purported to sell Greenacre to Able in 1950. Able then had an immediate cause of action against Owens for breach of the two present covenants.

However, the statute of limitations begins to run when the present covenant is breached. Since the present covenants were breached in 1950 and Able has not brought suit until the present, the usual statutory period of 4-6 years depending upon the jurisdiction, has run. Because his right to sue under the present covenants of warranty have passed, Able cannot now do so. However, his damages are minimal because he has obtained title to the property by adverse possession to be discussed infra.

As to the future covenants, Able will assert that those covenants are not breached until the grantee is actually or constructively evicted. The statute of limitations on future covenants does not begin to run until Able's possession is disturbed. There are no facts that Charlie has taken any active steps at present to disturb Able's occupancy of Greenacre. Until Charlie asserts a right of superior title to be discussed under Charlie's Rights, the statute of limitations will not begin to run. Able's rights to sue will be preserved until that time.

Assuming Charlie asserts his rights to Greenacre and seeks to oust Able, Able may sue Owens for breach of warranty of future covenants. A majority of jurisdictions will limit Able to damages for the $1,000.00 purchase price at the time of conveyance in 1950 plus interest and the costs to defend the title. A minority of jurisdictions will allow Able damages in the amount equal to the value of the land at time of eviction.

Adverse Possession

Adverse possession occurs when a true owner of land fails to take legal action to eject a possessor who claims adversely to the owner's interest under circumstances where possessor is hostile, open and notorious, actual and continuous for the statutory period.

Able will argue that at the time of the purported sale, he immediately recorded his deed and obtained an unsecured bank loan in order to make improvements on Greenacre. The true ownership was unknown to Able. Subjective intent is not required in most jurisdictions. Thus, his actions were based on a good faith belief of his ownership. As such, he was objectively in possession of Greenacre and his claim of right was without the grandfather's consent. Therefore, his possession was hostile to his grandfather's true and sole legal ownership.

In 1950, Able used the funds obtained from the bank loan to build a vacation cabin on the land. From that time to the present, he paid the taxes and allowed Bank to place a sign on the land at time of construction which read "Built with financing from Bank." Both the cabin and the sign remained in place, readily observable ever since. Even though Greenacre was inaccessible by road during six months each year due to snow, the grandfather could have determined Able's use during the remaining six months if he had wanted to defend his rights. Because Able made no attempt to conceal his use of Greenacre, such use was both open and notorious.

Further, Able lived in the cabin one month each summer when Greenacre was accessible by road. Such use was the type that would put the grandfather and other landowners in the community on reasonable notice that he was claiming possession as the actual owner.

Able lived one month each summer on the land in the above-described manner from 1950 to the present. This uninterrupted pattern of apparent vacationing, as any other mountain landowner might make, shows continuous possession for more than the usual 20 year common law statutory period.

Since Able entered Greenacre under color of title, and the grandfather failed to eject him, Able is deemed to be in adverse possession of the entire parcel described in his deed.

Able will qualify as an adverse possessor and claim exclusive rights to Greenacre.

II. CHARLIE'S RIGHTS TO GREENACRE

Recording Act - Bona Fide Purchaser For Value

Defined supra.

In 1973, Owens borrowed $5,000.00 from Charlie. As such, Charlie became a creditor. When he induced Owens to deed him Greenacre in 1978 in full satisfaction for that debt, he will assert that he became a subsequent purchaser.
Further, since the debt was then past due, it would constitute an antecedent debt, the extinguishment of which, in return for the deed, would qualify as valuable consideration.

Charlie will assert that he had no actual knowledge of Able's claim to Greenacre. Thus, he took without notice.

Greenacre was deeded to Charlie in the winter of 1978. Greenacre was inaccessible by road during this time due to snow. Therefore, it was impossible to make a reasonable search of the property. Able only used the property one month out of the year . As such, Charlie had no inquiry notice.

Able will counter that when he recorded his deed in 1950 and built a vacation cabin on the land, Charlie was on inquiry notice of Able's interest.

Finally, Charlie will argue that Able's deed was outside his chain of title. Able recorded before he came into actual possession of Greenacre. In a majority of jurisdictions, the deed was outside Charlie's chain of title. Therefore, even if he had conducted a search, Charlie would not have discovered the deed. He would not have constructive notice.

However, Able will rebut that the recording statute does not protect a subsequent purchaser without notice against prior interests that have arisen by operation of law. The recording statute stated "any unrecorded conveyance is deemed void as against a subsequent taker for value and without notice". Thus, Able's claim under adverse possession would still be valid. Able's interest arose by operation of law and not by "conveyance". The recording statute is inapplicable.

Prior-In-Time-Rule

Where a person does not come within the protection of the recording statute, the common law rule of first in time, first in right applies.

Owens purported to sell to Able in 1950. Able's rights to Greenacre were perfected in 1977 when, by operation of law, Owens' acquisition by will inured to the benefit of Able. This, Able's interest in Greenacre was "first in time" to Charlie's whose interest did not arise until Owens deeded Greenacre to him in 1978. Therefore, since Able was first in time, Charlie's claim will be subordinate to Able's "first in right" ownership.

Since the recording statute is inapplicable, Able will take Greenacre under the prior-in-time-rule.

REAL PROPERTY QUESTION #4

JOHN v. TED

Fred and Bob are next door neighbors. Both are friends and avid lawn bowlers. In 1940, they agreed while lawn bowling one morning, to put in lawn bowling lanes extending 15 feet onto each other's parcel from the boundary line between their parcels. Each agreed that the other could use the lanes anytime. At the same time, Bob told Fred that he could pick up to a basket of strawberries for himself from Bob's garden whenever Fred came over to lawn bowl. Bob memorialized his permission for Fred to pick strawberries on his bowling card.

Their parcels are located on sloping land with Fred's lot located above Bob's lot. Bob puts in a six foot retaining wall on his lot at the edge of the lawn bowling lanes so that a level course can be built by shoveling fill dirt against the wall up to the height of four feet. Both Fred and Bob put in many months of hard work leveling and preparing the lawn bowling lanes. Once the lanes were completed, Fred picked one basket of strawberries when in season every time he came over to bowl.

In 1960, Fred sells his parcel to his friend John with all rights, title and interest. John immediately began using the lawn bowling lanes and has since continued doing so on a regular basis on both parcels in question. He also has an affinity for strawberries and picks a case for himself and his pie shop during every bowling session. In that same year, Bob sells his parcel to his cousin, Ted. No mention was made in either deed of the lawn bowling lanes.

Ted hates most sports including lawn bowling. Finally, in 1970, Ted tells John to keep off his property and begins tearing out the lawn bowling lanes in order to put in a tulip field on the 15 foot portion of the lawn bowling lane located on his land. John counters by demanding that Ted remove the retaining wall to permit the surface water to flow into Ted's parcel. During frequent and heavy winter storms, water accumulates behind the wall and floods John's lot.

Assume a 10 year statute of limitations.

Discuss:

a) John's right to use the lawn bowling lanes on Ted's land.

b) John's right to go onto Ted's land to pick strawberries.

c) John's demand that Ted remove the retaining wall to permit the free flow of surface water.

IRAC OUTLINE SHEET

(I)	(R)	(A)	(C)

EXAMPLE OF PROPER IRAC OUTLINE

JOHN v. TED

(a) JOHN'S RIGHT TO USE LANES ON TED'S LAND

(I)	(R)	(A)	(C)
EXPRESS EASEMENT	Interest In Land Use Of Land	Fred & Bob are next door neighbors Both are friends & avid lawn bowlers In 1940, they agreed while lawn bowling to put lanes extending 15' onto each others parcel from the boundary line between their parcels. Each agreed that the other could use the lanes anytime	No Expressed Easement
	Writing Required	Each agreed Bob only memorialized Fred's permission to pick strawberries on his bowling card No mention made in either deed	
LICENSE	Permission To Use Of Land Limited Purpose	Agreed to put lanes in supra Agreed to let other use lanes anytime Other use lanes anytime supra	Valid License
IRREVOCABLE LICENSE	Substantial Improvements In Reliance	Bob & Fred's parcels located on sloping land with Fred's above Bob's Bob put up a 6' retaining wall on his lot at the edge of the lanes so that a level course could be built by shoveling dirt against the wall to a height of 4' Both Bob & Fred put in many months preparing the lanes	Valid Irrevocable License
	Licensor Estopped To Revoke	Fred sells his parcel to friend John Bob sells his parcel to cousin Ted Ted tells John to keep off his property	
TRANSFERABILITY OF A LICENSE	Non-Transferable Unless:	1960, Fred sells parcel to John with all rights, title and interest	
	Intent To Make Transferable	Fred an avid lawn bowler (intent to create easements?)	Transferable License
PRESCRIPTIVE EASEMENT	Use:		
	Hostile	1960, Fred sells parcel to John with all rights, title and interest John immediately began using lanes No mention was made in either deed (claim of right?/effect of license?)	Invalid Prescriptive Easement
	Open/Notorious	John immediately began using lanes on a regular basis	
	Actual Continuous	Using lanes on a regular basis supra John immediately began using and has since continued doing so on a regular basis 1960-1978	

(b) JOHN'S RIGHT TO PICK STRAWBERRIES

(I)	(R)	(A)	(C)
PROFIT	Right To Take Something Off Another's Land	1940 Bob told Fred that he could pick up to a basket of strawberries for himself from Bob's garden whenever Fred came over to bowl	Valid Profit
	Writing Required	Bob memorialized permission to pick strawberries on his bowling card	
PROFIT IN GROSS	No Benefit In Use Of Servient Tenement	1940 Bob told Fred that he could pick strawberries supra	Valid Profit In Gross
TRANSFERABILITY OF PROFITS IN GROSS	Non-Exclusive Profit Gross Not Transferable	1960 Fred sells parcel to John with all rights, title & interest Fred could pick strawberries supra	Not Transferable
TERMINATION OF PROFIT IN GROSS	Excessive Use Dominant Tenant Profit Extinguished	1940 Bob told Fred that he could pick strawberries up to one basket John has an affinity to strawberries & picks a case for himself & his pie shop during every bowling season	Profit In Gross Terminated

(c) JOHN'S DEMAND RE: RETAINING WALL

(I)	(R)	(A)	(C)
SURFACE WATER RIGHTS	Majority Rule: Natural Servitude Doctrine Common Law: Common Enemy Doctrine	1940, 6' retaining wall supra John demands Ted remove retaining wall to permit surface water to flow into Ted's parcel During frequent & heavy winter storms, water accumulated behind wall & floods John's lot	Jurisdictional Split

EXAMPLE OF IRAC REAL PROPERTY ISSUE

(I) **Surface Water Rights**

(R) A majority of jurisdictions follow the (1) natural servitude doctrine which provides that lower lands are servient to the natural flow and a landowner cannot obstruct or change the flow of surface water so as to injure others either above or below the obstruction. Common law jurisdictions have adhered to the (2) common enemy doctrine which holds that where surface water is involved, any landowner has an unqualified right to fend off surface waters by changing the drainage or building a dam.

(A) John will argue that the 6 foot retaining wall located on Ted's lot has interfered with the free flow of storm water down the sloping lots by causing heavy storm waters to accumulate behind the wall resulting in the flooding of his lot. Thus, John has a right under the (1) natural servitude doctrine to demand that Ted remove the retaining wall so that it will not continue to obstruct the free and natural flow of water down the sloping parcels. Since it is apparent that heavy storms do occur in the area on a frequent basis, Ted must act reasonably by removing the retaining wall so as to avoid flooding on John's parcel.

Ted will counter that winter storm waters that drain from John's parcel onto his land constitute surface waters. Under the (2) common enemy doctrine, Ted has an unqualified right to fend off these waters by leaving the retaining wall in place. The flooding of John's property has not been shown to create disproportionate harm since more than ten years have passed since the retaining wall was put in place. Neither Bob nor John ever complained during those 10 years. It can only be assumed that flooding occurred during the frequent heavy winter storms over that 10 year period and it was not until Ted decided to replace the lanes on his property with tulip fields that John registered his complaint. Absent a showing of disproportionate and unnecessary damage, John may not force Ted to remove the retaining wall.

(C) The jurisdictional rule applied will determine whether or not the retaining wall will have to be removed.

SUGGESTED MODEL ANSWER

A) JOHN'S RIGHT TO USE THE LAWN BOWLING LANES ON TED'S LAND

Express Easement

An express easement is an interest in land that entitles a person to use the land in possession of another and requires a writing to satisfy the Statute of Frauds.

Fred and Bob were friends and next door neighbors. They were both avid lawn bowlers. In 1940, Fred and Bob agreed, while lawn bowling one morning, to put lawn bowling lanes extending 15 feet onto each other's parcels. Each agreed that the other could use the lanes anytime. As such, they expressly agreed to give one another an interest in the use of the land where the lanes extended onto the other's parcel from the boundary line between their parcels.

However, since the agreement was made while Bob and Fred were bowling, the agreement appears to have been oral. No mention of the agreement was documented either on Bob's bowling card or in the deeds of conveyance when Bob and Fred sold their respective parcels. Absent a writing memorializing the agreement, the express easement will violate the Statute of Frauds.

No express easement was created.

License

A license is the granting of permission to go onto the land of another for a special or limited purpose.

Fred and Bob both agreed to let the other use the lawn bowling lanes on each other's property where they extended from the boundary lines between their parcels. Since permission was granted by each to go onto the land of the other for the special and limited purpose of lawn bowling, a license was created.

A valid license was established.

Irrevocable License

Where a licensee has constructed substantial improvements on the licensor's land in reliance on the license, the licensor is estopped from revoking the license until such time that the purpose of the license has terminated, or the licensee has amortized his investment, or after the purpose of making the investment ceases.

Bob and Fred's parcels are located on sloping land with Fred's above Bob's. Bob put up a 6 foot retaining wall on his lot at the edge of the bowling lanes so that a level course could be built by shoveling dirt against the wall to a height of 4 feet. Fred and Bob put in many months of hard work leveling and preparing the lawn bowling lanes. The expenditure of time and labor to construct such substantial improvements on both parcels in question was done in reliance on the agreement that

Bob and Fred could use the lanes on each other's land anytime for lawn bowling. Therefore, it would be unfair to John, a licensee as Fred's successor in interest to permit Ted, a licensor as Bob's successor in interest to revoke the license.

The license appears to be irrevocable until such time that the court determines that the purpose of the license has terminated or Fred/John have amortized their investment, or the purpose of making the investment has ceased.

Transferability Of A License

A license is usually presumed to be personal to the original licensee and nontransferable unless the licensor/licensee have the intent that it be made transferable.

John will assert that when Fred sold his parcel to him in 1960 with all rights, title and interest, Fred transferred both the property and all rights of use connected to it, including Fred's license to use Bob's parcel where the lawn bowling lanes extended onto it.

Tom will counter that a license is usually considered personal to the person who originally received it and, therefore, is nontransferable. Fred received permission to go onto the land in question because he was Bob's friend and an avid bowling neighbor. However, since Fred and Bob intended to create easements in each other's property which are transferable, the license created would not be too personal to transfer.

Therefore, the license is transferable.

Prescriptive Easement

A prescriptive easement is one implied in law where the use of another person's property is hostile, open and notorious, actual and continuous for the statutory period.

When John purchased Fred's parcel in 1960, he immediately began using the lawn bowling lanes on his and Bob's parcels. No mention of the use of the lawn bowling lanes was made in his deed. However, his deed contained the language "with all rights, title and interest". Since John apparently believed that this language inferred his use of the existing lanes was allowed on both parcels, despite lack of express permission from either Bob and later Ted, who purchased the parcel in question from Bob, John was doing so under claim of right.

Under the objective test, John would argue that his use of the lanes appeared to his adjoining neighbors to be done under a claim of right. Under the subjective test, John would argue that he believed, based on the location of the lawn bowling lanes and Fred's own prior use, that he had a right to use Ted's land for lawn bowling. However, since John had a license for the use of the lawn bowling lanes, there was no hostile use of the property. Thus, only if the license terminated in 1960 would hostility exist.

John used the lawn bowling lanes on a regular basis without attempting to conceal his use. He did so in a manner visible for all to see sufficient to put Ted on notice that John was claiming a right to use the lawn bowling lanes on Ted's property. Thus, John's use was open and notorious.

John's lawn bowling activities were carried out on a regular basis making his use actual.

Further, the regular use of the lanes in question from 1960-1978 demonstrates a continuous use for an 18 year period. Since that jurisdiction recognized a 10 year statute of limitations, John's use was continuous over the statutory period.

However, because the license was not terminated, there is no showing of hostile use. John is not entitled to a prescriptive easement to use the lanes on Ted's parcel.

B) JOHN'S RIGHT TO GO ONTO TED'S LAND TO PICK STRAWBERRIES

Profit

A profit is a right to take something off another person's land that is part of the land or a product of the land. A profit must be in writing in order to satisfy the Statute of Frauds.

As previously discussed, Fred and Bob agreed in 1940 that the other could use the lawn bowling lanes on the other's property anytime. At the same time, Bob told Fred that he could pick up to a basket of strawberries from Bob's garden whenever Fred came over to lawn bowl. Such an agreement created a right in Fred to take strawberries from Bob's garden, a product of Bob's land. Further, since Bob memorialized the oral agreement on his score card, this writing satisfies the Statute of Frauds.

A valid profit was created.

Profit In Gross

Where a profit does not benefit its owner in the use and enjoyment of the servient tenement but merely gives him the right to take something off the servient land, the profit is in gross.

Bob told Fred that Fred could pick up to a basket of strawberries from Bob's garden whenever he came over to lawn bowl. It does not appear that Bob meant that anyone who was his neighbor could take the strawberries. Instead, it appears that Bob meant that only his neighbor, Fred, could take the strawberries. Therefore, Fred received no benefit in the use and enjoyment of Bob's land which was the servient tenement. It merely gave Fred the right to come on Bob's land for the purpose of taking strawberries from Bob's garden. Since both Fred and Bob enjoyed the right to use the garden to pick strawberries, the profit in gross would be considered non-exclusive in nature.

John might counter that Bob may have meant that his neighbor (any person who lived next door, not necessarily Fred) would have a profit. In that case, the profit is appurtenant.

However, absent more facts regarding Bob's intent, it appears that a profit in gross was created.

Transferability Of Profits In Gross

A non-exclusive profit in gross is not ordinarily transferable.

When Fred sold his parcel to John in 1960, the conveyance included the language "with all rights, title and interest." Although Fred's rights included the profit concerning the strawberries. It was a non-exclusive profit in gross as previously discussed. This right was not transferable to John at the time of the sale because, to allow transferability would be to take away some of the potential profit from the servient estate holder.

Fred's profit was not transferable to John.

Termination Of Profits In Gross

Where excessive use by the dominant tenant is established, the profit will be extinguished.

When Bob told Fred he could pick strawberries, he expressly and unequivocally stated that this profit was to be limited to "up to one basket".

Even if John was determined to be Fred's successor in interest to the domient parcel, when John's affinity for the fruit compelled him to pick a case not only for himself but also for his pie shop, he exceeded the set use limitation. John's excessive strawberry picking went beyond the contemplation of the servient owner. Due to excessive use, the profit would be extinguished.

The profit in gross would have been terminated. John has no right to go on Ted's land to pick strawberries.

C. JOHN'S DEMAND THAT TED REMOVE THE RETAINING WALL

Surface Water Rights

A majority of jurisdictions follow the natural servitude doctrine which provides that lower lands are servient to the natural flow and a landowner cannot obstruct or change the flow of surface water so as to injure others either above or below the obstruction. Common law jurisdictions have adhered to the common enemy doctrine which holds that where surface water is involved, any landowner has an unqualified right to fend off surface waters by changing the drainage or building a dam.

John will argue that the 6 foot retaining wall located on Ted's lot has interfered with the free flow of storm water down the sloping lots by causing heavy storm waters to accumulate behind the wall resulting in the flooding of his lot. Thus, John has a right under the natural servitude doctrine to demand that Ted remove the retaining wall so that it will not continue to obstruct the free and natural flow of water down the sloping parcels. Since it is apparent that heavy storms do occur in the area on a frequent basis, Ted must act reasonably by removing the retaining wall so as to avoid flooding on John's parcel.

Ted will counter that winter storm waters that drain from John's parcel onto his land constitute surface waters. Under the common enemy doctrine, Ted has an unqualified right to fend off these waters by leaving the retaining wall in place. The flooding of John's property has not been shown to create disproportionate harm since more than ten years have passed since the retaining wall was put in place. Neither Bob nor John ever complained during those 10 years. It can only be assumed that flooding occurred during the frequent heavy winter storms over that 10 year period and it was not until Ted decided to replace the lanes on his property with tulip fields that John registered his complaint. Absent a showing of disproportionate and unnecessary damage, John may not force Ted to remove the retaining wall.

The jurisdictional rule applied will determine whether or not the retaining wall will have to be removed.

PROPERTY QUESTION #5

XAVIER v. ABEL

Owen owned a city block consisting of eight lots, each of which he had purchased from a different owner. In 1972, he conveyed by deed lots 1 and 2 to Xavier Corporation which built a department store thereon. The deed, which was promptly recorded, contained covenants by Owen for himself, his heirs, successors and assigns (1) to provide, maintain, repair and keep available on the remainder of the block for the non-exclusive use of customers of the department store a parking area for at least 500 automobiles and (2) to sell no tires or petroleum products on any of the remaining lots.

Owen then developed a shopping center with a 550-car parking lot on lots 3 through 8. In 1974, he sold the shopping center to Abel who had actual knowledge of the covenant restricting sale of tires and petroleum products but was unaware of the covenant about the parking lot.

A municipal zoning ordinance applicable to the area in which the shopping center is located prohibits free standing signs more than 15 feet high.

Abel now proposes to build a service station on the shopping center parking lot which will eliminate 100 parking spaces. A marketing survey reveals that unless the station has a 50 foot high free standing sign to attract customers from a nearby freeway, the service station will be unprofitable. A 15 foot sign will be barely visible from the adjoining streets.

(A) Can Xavier recover damages from Abel or prevent Abel from building the service station? Discuss.

(B) Assuming that Xavier cannot prevent Abel from building the service station, can the municipality prevent Abel from erecting a 50-foot sign in the parking area? Discuss.

IRAC OUTLINE SHEET

(I)	(R)	(A)	(C)

EXAMPLE OF PROPER IRAC OUTLINE

XAVIER (X) v. ABLE

(A) CAN X RECOVER DAMAGES OR PREVENT A FROM BUILDING SERVICE STATION?

1. MAINTENANCE OF 500 PARKING SPACES

(I)	(R)	(A)	(C)
AFFIRMATIVE COVENANT	Promise To Do	O owned city block of 8 lots each purchased from different owner In 1972 0 conveyed lots 1/2 to X which built a dept. store thereon Deed contained covenants by O to provide maintain, repair and keep available on remainder of block for non-exclusive use of customers of the dept. store a parking area for at least 500 autos	Affirmative Covenant
	Binds Promisor/Promisee Writing	O/X Deed	
BURDEN RUN WITH LAND	Covenant	Supra	
	Intent	1972 0 conveyed by deed promptly recorded for himself, his heirs, successors and assigns	
	Touch/Concern	To provide, etc. space for 500 autos (restrict use?)	Burden Runs
	Notice	O/X deed promptly recorded Lots 1/2 to X which built dept. store 1974 0 sold shopping center with its 550 car parking lot on lots 3-8 to A Unaware of covenant about the parking lot (constructive notice?) A had actual knowledge of covenant restricting sale of tires/petrol products	
	Privity Horizontal Vertical	O/X deed contained covenants for lots 1/2 and 3/8 O sold lots 3/8 to A	
	Writing	Deed	
DAMAGES	Diminution In Value	Proposed building of service station will eliminate 100 of 550 parking spaces	Damages Inadequate Seek Equity
EQUITABLE SERVITUDE	Covenant Notice Intent Touch/Concern	Supra Supra Supra Supra	Equitable Servitude
INJUNCTION-EQUITABLE SERVITUDE	Remedy In Equity	X seeks to prevent A from building station	Permitted
INADEQUATE LEGAL REMEDY	Equitable Relief Land Is Unique	O/X covenants parking area for at least 500/service station will eliminate 100 of the 550 parking spaces	Inadequate Legal Remedy
ENFORCEABILITY	Equity Acts In Personam	X/A before the court	Enforceable
IRREPARABLE HARM	Permanent/Irreparable Harm	Eliminate 100 of the 550 parking spaces	Irreparable Harm
PROPERTY RIGHT	Property/Personal Right	500 parking spaces	Property Right
HARDSHIPS	Balancing Unless Bad Faith	1972 provide at least 500 parking spaces for dept. store customers A had notice of a restriction preventing selling of tires/petroleum products	Hardships Balanced To X
TYPE OF INJUNCTION	TRO/Preliminary/Permanent	Eliminate 100 of 550 parking spaces supra	Injunction Granted

2. SALES OF TIRES/PETROLEUM PRODUCTS

(I)	(R)	(A)	(C)
NEGATIVE COVENANT	Promise Not To Do	O conveyed lots 1/2 to X Deed contained covenant to sell no tires or petrol products on any of the remaining lots 3-8	Negative Covenant
	Binds Promisor/Promisee	O/X	
BURDEN RUN WITH LAND	Covenant	Supra	Burden Runs With Land
	Intent Touch/Concern Notice	Supra Supra A had actual knowledge of the covenant restricting sale of tires/petrol products	
	Privity	Supra	
DAMAGES	Diminution In Value	Supra	Damages Inadequate Seek Equity
EQUITABLE SERVITUDE	Covenant Notice Intent Touch/Concern	Supra Supra Supra Supra	Equitable Servitude
INJUNCTION-EQUITABLE SERVITUDE	Supra	Supra	Supra
INADEQUATE LEGAL REMEDY	Equitable Relief Land Is Unique	Proposed service station/dept. store on lots 1/2 Selling of products (multiplicity of suits?)	Inadequate Legal Remedy
ENFORCEABILITY	Enforceable Decree	Supra	Enforceable
IRREPARABLE HARM	Permanent/Irreparable Harm	Proposed service station/dept. store on lots 1/2 (decrease in profits?)	Irreparable Harm
PROPERTY RIGHT	Property/Personal Right	Supra	Property Right
HARDSHIPS	Balancing Unless Bad Faith	A had actual knowledge (bad faith?)	No Balance
TYPE OF INJUNCTION	TRO/Preliminary/Permanent	Department store competition? (emergency?)	Injunction Granted

(B) CAN MUNICIPALITY PREVENT ABLE FROM ERECTING A 50 FOOT SIGN IN THE PARKING AREA?

(I)	(R)	(A)	(C)
ZONING-10TH AMENDMENT	Police Powers Health Safety Local Concern Welfare Aesthetics Environment Morals	A municipal ordinance applicable to the area in which the shopping center is located prohibits all free standing signs more than 15' high	Valid Zoning
COMPREHENSIVE PLAN	General Plan	Municipal ordinance applicable to area supra	Comprehensive Plan
	Applies To All Similarly Situated	Ordinance prohibits all free standing signs more than 15' high	
VARIANCE	Permits Relief For Non-Conforming Use Where: Practical Difficulty Substantial Hardship	Municipal ordinance applicable to area A now proposes to build a service station Marketing survey reveals that unless the station has a 50' high free standing sign to attract customers from a nearby fwy., service station will be unprofitable.	No Variance
FIFTH AMENDMENT	Gov't Taking Without Compensation	Municipal ordinance supra Marketing survey/without 50' sign, station unprofitable supra 15' sign will be barely visible from adjoining streets (other uses available?)	No Fifth Amendment Violation

EXAMPLE OF IRAC REAL PROPERTY ISSUE

(I) **Affirmative Real Covenant**

(R) An affirmative real covenant is a (1) promise to do a certain thing on land which (2) binds the promisee and promisor and requires a (3) writing.

(A) Owen owned a city block consisting of 8 lots each purchased from a different owner. In 1972, Owen conveyed lots 1 and 2 to Xavier Corporation which built a department store thereon. The deed contained a covenant to provide, maintain, repair and keep available on the remainder of the block at least 500 parking spaces. This language demonstrated Owen's affirmative (1) promise to keep these spaces available on lots 3-8 for the non-exclusive use of Xavier's department store customers. Xavier was the original (2) promisee. Owen was the original promisor. Both parties were bound by the promise. The deed itself satisfies the requirement for a (3) writing.

(C) Therefore, an affirmative real covenant was created.

SUGGESTED MODEL ANSWER

(A) CAN X RECOVER DAMAGES OR PREVENT A FROM BUILDING THE SERVICE STATION?

1. MAINTENANCE OF 500 PARKING SPACES

Affirmative Real Covenant

An affirmative real covenant is a promise to do a certain thing on land which binds the promisee and promisor and requires a writing.

Owen owned a city block consisting of 8 lots each purchased from a different owner. In 1972, Owen conveyed lots 1 and 2 to Xavier Corporation which built a department store thereon. The deed contained a covenant to provide, maintain, repair and keep available on the remainder of the block at least 500 parking spaces. This language demonstrated Owen's affirmative promise to keep these spaces available on lots 3-8 for the non-exclusive use of Xavier's department store customers. Xavier was the original promisee. Owen was the original promisor. Both parties were bound by the promise. The deed itself satisfies the requirement for a writing.

Therefore, an affirmative real covenant was created.

Does the Covenant's Burden Run With the Land?

For the burden to run with the land, the contracting parties must show a covenant, intent to bind all subsequent heirs and assigns, the promise touches and concerns the land, the parties have notice and are in privity.

The Owen/Xavier covenant has been previously established. Owen conveyed the property to Xavier in 1972. The deed of conveyance was promptly recorded and contained the language "by Owen for himself, his heirs, successors and assigns." This express language demonstrates the intent of the contracting parties to bind all subsequent heirs and assigns.

The promise to maintain at least 500 parking spaces would act to diminish the value (burden) of lots 3-8 because it would restrict its use for other purposes. Conversely, the promise would enhance the value (benefit) of Xavier's land by assuring it with available parking for its department store. As such, the promise touches and concerns the land.

The promise contained in the Owen/Xavier deed was promptly recorded. In 1974, Owen sold the shopping center with its 550-car parking lot on lots 3-8 to Abel. Abel was unaware of the covenant concerning the parking lot and will assert that he had no actual knowledge. Xavier's deed for lots 1 and 2 would not be in Abel's chain of title. Therefore, even if he had searched his chain of title, he would not have discovered Xavier's deed in order to be put on constructive notice of the covenant.

However, Abel had knowledge of the covenant restricting the sale of tires and petroleum products. Since lots 1 and 2 and lots 3-8 had a shopping center, he should be charged with the responsibility of inquiring whether there were further covenants in existence. The lay of the land should have put Abel on inquiry notice to search the deeds concerning the 1 and 2 neighboring lots. His lack of diligence would not excuse his responsibility to do so and in some jurisdictions, he would be deemed to have had inquiry notice. In other jurisdictions, these facts would not be considered sufficient for a showing of notice.

Finally, Owen and Xavier were the original covenanting parties. This grantor/grantee relationship created mutual interests in lots 3-8 regarding the maintenance of the 500 parking spaces establishing horizontal privity of estate.

When Abel purchased lots 3-8 from Owen, he would be classified as a successive assignee to Owen, who was one of the original parties to the promise. As such, he would be in vertical privity.

The burden of maintaining 500 parking spaces runs with the land.

Remedy Damages

The measure of property damages is the diminution in value.

Xavier's land will undoubtedly diminish in value if 100 of the existing 550 shopping center parking spaces are decreased. He will be entitled to the difference between the value before and after the removal of the spaces.

However, it may be to Xavier's advantage to enjoin the removal rather than to merely seek damages. Therefore, he must seek his remedy in equity.

Equitable Servitude

An equitable servitude is a covenant that equity will enforce against assignees of the burdened land who have notice of the covenant upon a showing of intent and touch and concern.

As discussed supra, a covenant did exist between Owen and Xavier. Further, in those jurisdictions who would charge Abel with inquiry notice, as discussed supra, Abel would be on notice of the restriction. Also, a showing of intent and touch and concern has been established previously. Therefore, Xavier could enforce an equitable servitude.

Injunction - Equitable Servitude

Xavier may seek the remedy of an injunction based on theory of the equitable servitude.

Inadequacy of Legal Remedy

The court must find that the legal remedies available to the plaintiff are inadequate in order to allow equitable relief.

Abel's proposed service station will result in a loss of 100 of the existing 550 parking spaces. Since Xavier was promised at least 500 spaces for the non-exclusive use of his department store customers, he has an interest in the land designated for parking. As land is unique, monetary damages cannot adequately compensate him for this loss.

Thus, there appears to be no adequate remedy at law available.

Enforceability

The equitable remedy sought must be enforceable as equity acts in personam.

Since both parties appear to be before the court, the equity court will have the power to enforce a binding in personam decision.

The court's decree is enforceable.

Irreparable Harm

The plaintiff must establish a permanent, irreparable harm that will result if injunctive relief is not granted.

Adequate parking facilities are essential to attract and maintain customer trade. Xavier's department store business could be severely harmed if his customers are not provided with adequate parking. A loss of 100 parking spaces will result in lost business constituting permanent, irreparable harm.

Irreparable harm can be established.

Property Right

At common law, a property right had to be at issue to qualify for injunctive relief. Modernly, a personal right may be involved.

Here, Xavier's right to the use of at least 500 parking spaces is at issue. Thus, a property right is involved.

Balancing of Hardships

Where there is no evidence of bad faith on the part of the defendant, the court will balance the hardships of the parties.

Xavier built its department store in 1972 relying on the covenant that a minimum of 500 parking spaces for its customers would be provided on lots 3-8. The loss of 100 existing spaces will decrease the customer parking to 450 spaces. As such, Xavier will lose the necessary parking facilities for customers. This could result in the financial hardship of lost business.

Abel will argue that, as a landowner, he has the right to develop his property. If he is denied this right and, instead, forced to maintain all 500 parking spaces, he will suffer the hardship.

However, Able had notice of the restriction before he sought to violate it. He knew he had no right to develop a service station that sold tires and petroleum products. Therefore, he cannot now claim a hardship for failing to comply with existing restrictions of which he was aware. To do so would be an act of bad faith.

Since Xavier appears to have the more compelling argument, the court will balance the hardship in its favor.

Type of Injunction

The court may issue a temporary restraining order (TRO) in an emergency situation, or it may wait until after trial or a hearing to grant a preliminary and/or permanent injunction.

Xavier will assert that the denial of the parking spaces in question creates an emergency situation to his business. If immediate relief is not granted, great financial loss could result before a hearing is held.
It appears that the court would grant a TRO. After a trial, the court may also grant a preliminary and then a permanent injunction prohibiting the building of the service station.

2. SALE OF TIRES AND PETROLEUM PRODUCTS

Negative Real Covenant

A negative real covenant is a promise not to do a certain thing on land which binds the promisee and promisor and requires a writing.

When Owen conveyed lots 1 and 2 to Xavier, the deed contained a covenant to sell no tires or petroleum products on any of the remaining 3-8 lots. This was a promise not to engage in any business that would involve the sale of the above-mentioned products on the remaining land. Xavier was the original promisee. Owen was the original promisor. Both parties were bound by the promise. The deed satisfies the requirement for a writing.

Therefore, a negative real covenant was created.

Does the Covenant's Burden Run With the Land?

Defined supra.

The covenant, intent, touch and concern and privity have been previously established. In this instance, Abel had actual knowledge of the covenant restricting these sales constituting sufficient notice.

The burden runs with the land.

Remedy - Damages

Defined and discussed supra.

Equitable Servitude

Defined and discussed supra.

Injunction - Equitable Servitude

Defined and discussed supra.

Inadequacy of Legal Remedy

Defined supra.

If Abel builds the service station on his property and subsequently sells tires and petroleum products, continuous competition with Xavier's stores would occur. This would force Xavier to sue Abel for breach of contract upon every sale of tires and petroleum products from Abel's service station, resulting in a multiplicity of suits.

Therefore, monetary damages would be an inadequate remedy at law.

Enforceability

Defined and discussed supra.

Irreparable Harm

Defined supra.

If Abel is allowed to sell tires and petroleum products, he may be in direct competition with the stores in Xavier's shopping center. This could decrease profits from those store operators causing permanent, irreparable harm.

Irreparable harm can be established.

Property Right

Defined and discussed supra.

Balancing of the Hardship

Defined supra.

Abel had actual notice of the covenant in question. Since the scope and duration of the covenant appears reasonable, Abel's attempt to violate it by building a service station where tires and petroleum products will undoubtedly be sold is an exercise of bad faith.

The court will not balance the hardships for Abel.

Type of Injunction

Defined supra.

Xavier will assert that the anticipated competition from the building of the service station will create an emergency marketing situation for its department store tenants. If immediate relief is not granted, great financial loss could result before a hearing is held.

It appears that the court would grant a TRO. After a trial, the court may grant a preliminary and then a permanent injunction preventing the building of the service station.

(B) CAN THE MUNICIPALITY PREVENT ABEL FROM ERECTING A 50 FOOT SIGN IN THE PARKING AREA?

Zoning - Tenth Amendment

The police powers of the Tenth Amendment of the United States Constitution reserves to the states the right to regulate the health, safety, local concern, welfare, aesthetics, environment, and morals of their citizens.

The municipal ordinance prohibits all free standing signs more than 15 feet high in the area where the shopping center is located. If the purpose of the ordinance is to eliminate the distractions that these signs create to motorists on a nearby freeway, the ordinance would impact on driver safety and the local concern regarding traffic control. Further, signs in excess of 15 feet can create an eyesore which affects the aesthetics in the surrounding environment.

Therefore, the purpose of the ordinance clearly falls within acceptable police powers reserved to the State through the 10th Amendment.

Comprehensive Plan

A zoning plan must be based on a general plan which is internally consistent and applies to all landowners similarly situated.

As shown, the purpose of the ordinance is to improve the safety and environment for the municipality's citizens. The ordinance provides for this public need which is best served by such a restriction. It appears to be based on a general plan which is internally consistent to the area in its application.

Further, the municipal ordinance prohibits all free standing signs more than 15 feet high in the shopping center area. Since it applies equally to all landowners/occupiers similarly situated in this area, it does not discriminate.

Therefore, the ordinance is based on a comprehensive plan.

Variance

A valid zoning plan requires a variance for non-conforming uses that existed at the time of the ordinance to permit relief where the restrictions contained in the ordinance cause the owner practical difficulty or substantial hardship.

The municipal ordinance applicable to the area in question was apparently in effect before Abel decided to build a service station and erect the 50 foot sign meant to attract customers. The non-conforming 50 foot sign that he now proposes to build as a result of his marketing profitability study did not exist before the enactment of the ordinance.

Further, although a marketing survey has revealed that, unless the station has a 50 foot sign, it will be unprofitable, any practical difficulty or substantial hardship is outweighed by the fact that the sign was not in existence before enactment of the ordinance. Xavier should not be rewarded for knowingly attempting to violate an existing ordinance of which he had notice.

The municipality need not consider awarding a variance to Abel for relief from the restriction.

A variance will not be allowed.

Fifth Amendment

The Fifth Amendment prohibits a government taking without compensation.

Abel will assert that if the ordinance acts to deny the right to erect the 50 foot sign, he will be unable to attract service station customers from the freeway as revealed by a marketing survey. The prohibition of the sign to 15 feet will make his business barely visible from adjoining streets depriving him of its profitable use. Therefore, the municipal ordinance will act as a government taking of his potential business profits without compensation.

However, the use of the land for a service station is not the only use that Abel may pursue. The land can be used for parking facilities for the nearby shopping centers and could generate profits if properly managed. Moreover, the ordinance was in existence before Able sought to violate it. Abel knew when he bought the land that a sign of that height was not permitted. Thus, since other reasonable uses are available and because the erection of the 50 foot sign violated an existing ordinance the ordinance will not constitute a government taking.

The Fifth Amendment is not violated. The municipality can prevent Abel from building the 50 foot sign in the parking area.

*CAVEAT: Due to the racehorse nature of this examination, student answer may be conclusary in the injunction analysis unlike the model answer.

SECTION VII

EVIDENCE

EVIDENCE

LEARN TO WRITE . . . THE RIGHT WAY®

EVIDENCE QUESTION #1

STATE v. TIM

Tim was tried in a State A court for possession of 1/10 gram of heroin, a felony. The government's only witness was Officer Jenks, an undercover police officer. Jenks testified after Tim arranged to sell drugs to Jenks, Tim, in company with Sue, met Jenks on September 13, 1984. Jenks also testified that Tim refused to make the sale, and that Jenks arrested Tim, searched him, and found a substance he believed to be heroin in Tim's jacket pocket.

1) The prosecutor then offered as an exhibit a document entitled "Official State A Forensic Laboratory Report," which states that the unknown substance found in possession of Tim was tested and found to be heroin. The report concludes: "I certify that the above is a true and accurate statement of the findings of this state agency as made this date" and is signed by A. Smith, Executive Director and Custodian (seal).

2) As its first witness, the defense called the defendant, Tim, who testified on direct that he was in possession only of powdered milk and that he was being framed by Jenks. On cross-examination, Tim was asked, "Isn't it true that on May 1, 1983, you were in possession of 1/2 gram of heroin?" Over defense objection, Tim was instructed by the court to answer and said "yes."

3) As its second witness, the defense called Sue, who testified: that she had been dating the defendant for a year, that on the eight occasions they dined out prior to the offense, he always drank his coffee after having added powdered milk taken from a jacket pocket.

4) Sue then testified: that Jenks once arrested her for prostitution and offered to release her on payment of a bribe; that when she refused, Jenks said, "Just wait, I'll get you and all your friends."

5) In rebuttal, the prosecution called Dr. Walt, MD., who testified: that on September 9, 1984, he examined Tim, who complained of insomnia and anxiety; that during the private examination Tim stated that he was a narcotics addict in need of money to supply his habit; and that Tim asked Dr. Walt if he would like to buy drugs.

Assume that all appropriate objections were made. Were the items of evidence (1) through (5) properly admitted? Discuss. In dealing with item (2), discuss only the cross-examination and ignore the defendant's privilege against self-incrimination.

IRAC OUTLINE SHEET

(I)	(R)	(A)	(C)

EXAMPLE OF PROPER IRAC OUTLINE

STATE v. TIM (T)

(1) LABORATORY REPORT

(I)	(R)	(A)	(C)
LOGICAL RELEVANCE	Tendency In Reason To Prove/Disprove Disputed Fact	Exhibit document entitled official State A Forensic laboratory report states the unknown substance found in T's possession was tested/found to be heroin	Logically Relevant
	Consequence To Action	T tried in State A for possession of 1/10 gram of heroin, a felony	
AUTHENTICATION	Proponent Must Present Evidence Of Chain Of Custody	J arrested T/searched him Substance in T's pocket Report concludes I certify that the above is a true and accurate STATEENT of the findings of this state agency as made this date/signed by A. Smith, Executive & Custodian (seal)	Authenticated
HEARSAY	Out-Of-Court Statement	Official State A Forensic lab report	
	Offered For Truth Of Matter Asserted	States substance found in T's possession tested/found to be heroin	Hearsay
EXCEPTION-OFFICIAL RECORD	Written Statement	Document	
	Public Official	A. Smith Executive Director & Custodian	Arguable
	Duty To Record	Executive Director & Custodian	
	Personal Knowledge	Lab report signed by A. Smith	
EXCEPTION-BUSINESS RECORD	Kept Within Regular Course Of Business	Official State A Forensic Lab Report	
	Entrant Has Personal Knowledge	Report signed by A. Smith	
	Business Duty to Report	Substance tested/official lab report supra	
	Entry Made At/Near Time Of Event	Findings as of this date Substance tested/official lab report supra	Arguable
	Trustworthy	Official Forensic Lab report "I certify"	

(2) TESTIMONY OF TIM

(I)	(R)	(A)	(C)
LOGICAL RELEVANCE	Tendency In Reason To Prove/Disprove Disputed Fact	On cross x, isn't it true that on 5/1/83 you were in possession of 1/2 gram of heroin T answered yes	Logically Relevant
	Consequence To Action	T arranged to sell drugs to J/ met 9/13/84 T tried In State A for possession of 1/10 gram of heroin	
CROSS-EXAMINATION-SCOPE	Common Law-Unrestricted	Defense called T who testified on direct	
	Federal Rules- Matters Put In Issue On Direct Including Credibility	He was in possession only of powdered milk/being framed by J On cross, T asked re 5/1/83 possession 1/2 gram of heroin (leading question?) Over defense objection,T instructed by court to answer/said "Yes"	Beyond Scope Of Cross-Examination
PRIOR BAD ACTS	F.R. Allow Cross-Examination Into Any Prior Bad Acts Pertinent To Truthfulness / Veracity	5/1/83 T in possession of 1/2 gram of heroin/T said Yes Possession	Improper Impeachment
CHARACTER EVIDENCE	Bad Character To Prove Propensity	5/1/83 T in possession 1/2 gram of heroin T said yes	
	Defendant Must Open The Door	Prosecution introduced evidence	Improper Character

(3) SUE'S (S) TESTIMONY RE: POWDERED MILK

(I)	(R)	(A)	(C)
LOGICAL RELEVANCE	Tendency In Reason To Prove/Disprove Disputed Fact	S testified that she had been dating T for a year; on 8 occasions they dined out prior to the offense, T always drank coffee after having added powdered milk taken jacket pocket	Logically Relevant
	Consequence To Action	T tried in state A for possession of 1/10 gram heroin/substance believed to be heroin taken from T's jacket pocket by J T testified that he was being framed by J	
LAY OPINION	Common Law-Prohibited Modern Law-Admissible		
	Personal Observations/Facts In Dispute No Better Evidence	8 occasions T drank coffee after having added powdered milk supra	Proper Lay Opinion
CHARACTER EVIDENCE	Bad Character To Prove Propensity	T always drank coffee after having added powdered milk from jacket pocket	Improper Character
	Defendant Must Open The Door	(specific act)	
HABIT EVIDENCE	Routine/Repeated Response	On the 8 occasions they dined out prior to the offense, T always drank his coffee after having added powdered milk supra	Proper Habit
	Protracted Period Of Time	S had been dating T for a year/8 occasions they dined out prior to offense	

(4) SUE'S (S) TESTIMONY RE J'S THREAT TO GET HER 8 HER FRIEND

(I)	(R)	(A)	(C)
LOGICAL RELEVANCY	Tendency In Reason To Prove/Disprove Disputed Fact	T said J was framing him J once arrested S for prostitution & offered to release her on payment of bribe When S refused, J said "Just wait, I'll get you and all your friends"	Logically Relevant
	Consequence To Action	T's felony arrest supra	
HEARSAY	Out-Of-Court Statement	J once arrested S supra/offered to release her for bribe/Just wait...supra	Hearsay
	Offered For Truth Of Matter Asserted	T being framed? (bias)	
DECLARATIONS OF PRESENT STATE OF MIND TO SHOW SUBSEQUENT CONDUCT	Out Of Court Declaration	J arrested S supra	Arguable
	Present State Of Mind At Issue	J said just wait I'll get you and all your friends supra	
	Probability Of Subsequent Act	J framed T?	

(5) DR. WALT'S TESTIMONY RE TIM'S PHYSICAL CONDITION

a) Complaints Of Insomnia/Anxiety

(I)	(R)	(A)	(C)
LOGICAL RELEVANCE	Tendency In Reason To Prove/Disprove Disputed Fact	9-9-84 Dr. W examined T	Logically Relevant
	Consequence To Action	Complained insomnia/anxiety	
HEARSAY	Out-Of-Court Statement	Complaints at Dr. W s office	
	Offered For Truth of Matter Asserted	Heroin user?	Hearsay
EXCEPTION-STATE OF BODY	Physical Condition At Issue	During medical examination	Valid Exception
	Spontaneous Statements To Prove Condition	Complaints	
PHYSICIAN/PATIENT PRIVILEGE	Doctor/Patient Relationship	Dr. W examined T	Invalid Privilege
	Confidential Information	Complaints during medical examination	
	Info Related To Treatment	Complaints	
	Majority Not Applicable In Criminal Proceeding	State v Tim	

b) T's Statement "I Am A Narcotics User"

(I)	(R)	(A)	(C)
LOGICAL RELEVANCE	Tendency In Reason To Prove/Disprove Disputed Fact	Narcotics addict	Logically Relevant
	Consequence To Action	Needed $ to supply habit Arrest for heroin possession	
HEARSAY	Out-Of-Court Statement	Supra	Hearsay
	Offered For Truth Of Matter Asserted	Supra	
EXCEPTION-ADMISSION	Asserts Belief Inconsistent With Position At Trial	Narcotics addict in need of $ Not in possession	Valid Exception
PHYSICIAN/PATIENT PRIVILEGE	Doctor/Patient Relationship	Supra	Partial Privilege Minority Of Jurisdictions
	Confidential Information	Narcotics user	
	Info Related To Treatment	Addiction needs $	

c) T's Offer To Sell Drugs

(I)	(R)	(A)	(C)
LOGICAL RELEVANCE	Tendency In Reason To Prove/Disprove Disputed Fact	Offered to sell Dr. W drugs	Logically Relevant
	Consequence To Action	Heroin possession	
HEARSAY	Offered For Truth Of Matter Asserted	Supra	Hearsay
	Truth Of Matter Asserted	Heroin possession	
EXCEPTION-ADMISSION	Asserts Belief Inconsistent With Position At Trial	Supra	Valid Exception
PHYSICIAN/PATIENT PRIVILEGE	Doctor/Patient Relationship	Supra	No Privilege
	Confidential Information	Offer to sell drugs	
	Info Related To Treatment	Supra	
LEGAL RELEVANCE	Probative v Prejudicial	Heroin possession Selling	Not Legally Relevant

EXAMPLE OF IRAC EVIDENCE ISSUE

(I) **Exception - Business Record**

(R) Business records kept (1) within the regular course of business activity may be admitted if (2) the entrant has personal knowledge, had a (3) business duty to report, (4) the entry was made at or near the time of the event, and (5) the records are trustworthy.

(A) As stated previously, the Official State A forensic lab report was signed by A. Smith who was acting (1) within the regular course of his official business duties. However, there is no showing that (2) A. Smith had (3) personal knowledge of the findings. As an Official State A Forensic Laboratory, it appears that those persons responsible for testing the substance had a business duty to report their findings. It appears that the findings were (4) entered at or near the time they were made.

Further, it was an official forensic lab report signed by the Executive Director and certified under seal. Absent facts to the contrary, (5) the facts related to the lab report records indicate a showing of trustworthiness.

(C) Depending upon whether A. Smith had personal knowledge of the report's contents so will determine whether the report will qualify as a business record exception.

SUGGESTED MODEL ANSWER

STATE v. TIM

1) PROSECUTION'S INTRODUCTION OF OFFICIAL FORENSIC LABORATORY REPORT

Logical Relevance

Evidence is logically relevant if it has any tendency in reason to prove or disprove a disputed fact of consequence to the determination of the action.

The exhibit document entitled Official State A Forensic Laboratory Report states that the unknown substance found in Tim's possession was tested and found to be heroin. This conclusion has a tendency in reason to prove that the substance taken from Tim was heroin, a disputed fact of consequence to the determination of the felony possession action.

The report is logically relevant.

Authentication - Chain of Custody

Where real evidence that is not of the type easily recognized, or is capable of causing confusion or subject to tampering, the proponent of the object must present evidence of its chain of custody.

Jenks testified that he arrested Tim, he searched him and found a substance he believed to be heroin in Tim's pocket. However, the prosecution did not present evidence that the substance Jenks took from Tim's jacket pocket was actually that which was analyzed by the Forensic Laboratory. Since there was no showing that the chain of custody was adequately maintained in order to protect against substitution or tampering, the report alone is insufficient to prove that the conclusions in the report were a result of testing the actual substance taken from Tim.

Further, the prosecution failed to introduce expert testimony that the testing procedures used by the Forensic Lab were conducted by qualified experts in the field or that the testing procedures were reliable. An official report certifying the statement of the findings of this state agency signed by A. Smith may be insufficient for this foundational requirement.

The report did contain the signature of A. Smith, Executive Director and Custodian of the lab under seal. If the court deems the lab a recognized government department and A. Smith an authorized signatory, the court, in its discretion, may receive the report into evidence without independent proof of authenticity.

It appears the report has been properly authenticated.

Hearsay

Hearsay is an out-of-court statement offered to prove the truth of the matter asserted.

The report was prepared at the State A Forensic Laboratory, outside the present proceeding. As such, it is considered an out-of-court statement. It is being offered to prove that the substance found in Tim's possession and tested by the lab was heroin, the truth of the matter asserted.

The report is inadmissible hearsay.

Exception - Official Record

Documents prepared by a public official who has a duty to record the document within the scope of his/her official duties will act as an exception to hearsay where the recording is based on the official's personal knowledge of the facts recorded.

The report was in the form of a written document. It was ostensibly prepared and signed by A. Smith. As a public official acting in the capacity of Executive Director and Custodian, A. Smith would be charged with the duty to record results of the testing procedures concerning substances turned over to it for analysis.

However, it is not clear whether A. Smith had personal knowledge of the results of the testing procedures. He may have simply signed the report after other state agency employees actually made the findings. Absent Smith's personal knowledge, the report will not qualify as an official record.

Official record is an invalid exception.

Exception - Business Record

Business records kept within the regular course of business activity may be admitted if the entrant has personal knowledge, had a business duty to report, the entry was made at or near the time of the event, and the records are trustworthy.

As stated previously, the Official State A forensic lab report was signed by A. Smith who was acting within the regular course of his official business duties. However, there is no showing that A. Smith had personal knowledge of the findings.

As an Official State A Forensic Laboratory, it appears that those persons responsible for testing the substance had a business duty to report their findings. It appears that the findings were entered at or near the time they were made.

Further, it was an official forensic lab report signed by the Executive Director and certified under seal. Absent facts to the contrary, the facts related to the lab report records indicate a showing of trustworthiness.

Depending upon whether A. Smith had personal knowledge of the report's contents so will determine whether the report will qualify as a business record exception.

2) TIM'S TESTIMONY RE: POSSESSION OF POWDERED MILK/FRAME BY JENKS

Logical Relevance

Defined supra.

On cross-examination, the prosecution asked Tim if it wasn't true that he'd been in possession of one half gram of heroin on May 1, 1983. Tim answered "Yes". Tim's affirmative response has a tendency in reason to prove that he regularly kept heroin on his person for purposes of sale, a disputed fact of consequence to the determination of the current felony possession action.

Tim's testimony is logically relevant.

Cross-Examination - Scope

Common law permits unrestricted cross-examination. However, the federal rules restrict cross-examination to any matter related to a subject raised on direct examination including the witness' credibility.

In common law jurisdictions, the prosecution's question concerning Tim's previous May 1, 1983 heroin possession would be permissible since the subject matter of cross-examination was unrestricted. However, under the federal rules, the prosecution is restricted to cross-examination only on matters raised on direct examination. Since the defense's direct examination dealt only with subject matter concerning powdered milk and Jenks' attempt to frame Tim, the prosecution may not examine on subject matter concerning a May 1, 1983 heroin possession charge unrelated to Tim's statement that he was in possession only of powdered milk. The form of the prosecution question is not objectionable. Leading questions are allowed on cross-examination. However, the content of the question is inadmissible as is Tim's answer "Yes".

Under the federal rules, the cross-examination question and answer should be stricken as beyond the scope of proper cross-examination.

Impeachment - Character for Honesty

Prior Bad Acts

The federal rules allow the court, within their discretion, to permit cross-examination of prior bad acts for purposes of impeachment of a witness if the act is pertinent to truthfulness or veracity.

The prosecution's cross-examination asked about Tim's act of being found in possession of 1/2 gram of heroin. The question of Tim's heroin possession shows an act of poor moral character. It is not pertinent to truthfulness or veracity.

Tim's testimony was improper impeachment testimony.

Character Evidence

The prosecution may not introduce evidence of the defendant's bad character to prove his propensity to commit the crime charged unless the defendant has first opened the door to his own character.

The prosecution asked Tim if he had been in possession of heroin on May 1, 1983 to which he responded "yes". The prosecution was offering evidence of Tim's bad character from prior testimony to prove Tim's propensity to commit the crime for which he is charged. Such evidence would prove the likelihood that Tim acted in conformity with that trait when Tim's September 13, 1984 arrest resulted in the seizure of heroin on his person.

However, it was the prosecution who introduced this evidence. The defendant has not first opened the door to his own character. It appears that the prosecution is simply trying to prove that Tim had a propensity to commit the crime with which he is presently charged. Tim's admission would appear to confuse the jury or mislead it into believing that, because he was in possession of heroin more than a year earlier, he probably was guilty on this occasion.

Tim's testimony is improper character evidence.

3) SUE'S TESTIMONY RE: POWDERED MILK

Logical Relevancy

Defined supra.

Sue testified that she had been dating Tim for a year. During the eight times they had dined out prior to the arrest, Tim had always drank coffee after having added powdered milk taken from his jacket pocket. Such testimony has a tendency in reason to prove that the substance Jenks took from Tim's pocket on September 13, 1984 was powdered milk, a disputed fact of consequence to the determination of whether Tim was being framed by Jenks on a false charge or was in possession for purposes of the felony action.

Sue's testimony is logically relevant.

Lay Opinion

Common law prohibited lay opinion. Modernly, lay opinion will be admissible when it is a result of that witness' personal observation of facts in dispute and when no better evidence can be reasonably obtained.

Sue testified that she'd been with Tim on eight occasions when she'd personally observed him drink coffee after having added powdered milk taken from his jacket pocket. She testified that the substance was powered milk. Under common law, her testimony was prohibited.

Modernly, the <u>use</u>, <u>smell</u> and <u>appearance</u> of powdered milk is something about which normal persons regularly form opinions. Sue testified that the substance was powered milk based on her <u>personal</u> <u>observations</u>. Her testimony is <u>helpful</u> to the jury in its <u>determination</u> as to whether the substance taken from Tim was actually powdered <u>milk</u> or <u>heroin</u>. It appears that <u>no</u> <u>better</u> <u>evidence</u> can be reasonable obtained to dispute her observations.

Therefore, Sue's testimony is proper lay opinion.

<u>Character Evidence</u>

Defined supra.

Sue's <u>testimony</u> is offered to <u>prove</u> that, since Tim had a <u>propensity</u> to <u>carry</u> powdered <u>milk</u> in his jacket pocket on numerous occasions before the arrest, he was <u>acting</u> in <u>conformity</u> with that trait on September 13, 1984 when Jenks removed the substance from Tim's jacket pocket.

However, since Sue is testifying to <u>specific</u> <u>instances</u> of Tim's conduct rather than opinion or reputation, her testimony is <u>inadmissible</u>.

Sue's testimony is improper character evidence.

<u>Habit Evidence</u>

Habit evidence is admissible if a <u>particular</u> activity, <u>routine</u> or response is <u>frequently</u> <u>repeated</u> over a <u>protracted</u> <u>period</u> of <u>time</u>.

Tim's <u>use</u> of powdered <u>milk</u> taken from his jacket pocket and added to his coffee on every occasion that Sue dined with him was a <u>routine</u> response <u>frequently</u> <u>repeated</u> whenever Tim had coffee.

Further, Sue's observations spanned <u>eight</u> occasions over the period of one year. Most courts would find this time frame sufficient to prove a protracted <u>period</u> of <u>time</u>.

Sue's testimony is proper habit evidence.

4) <u>SUE'S TESTIMONY RE: JENKS THREAT TO GET SUE AND HER FRIENDS</u>

<u>Logical Relevancy</u>

Defined supra.

Sue's testimony that Jenks once arrested her for prostitution, and then offered to release her on payment of a bribe, followed by a <u>threat</u> to get her and her friends when she refused has a <u>tendency</u> in reason to <u>prove</u> that her refusal motivated Jenks to <u>frame</u> her friends. Tim has testified that Jenks was framing him. Jenks' motivation for revenge through perjured testimony is a <u>disputed</u> <u>fact</u> of <u>consequence</u> to the <u>determination</u> of Tim's guilt or innocence on the felony <u>action</u>.

Sue's testimony is logically relevant.

Hearsay

Defined supra.

Sue's testimony involved a conversation she'd had with Jenks outside the present proceeding. Thus, it was an out-of-court statement. It is being offered to prove that Jenks had a motive to perjure his testimony in order to frame her friend Tim, the truth of the matter asserted.

Sue's testimony is inadmissible hearsay.

Exception - Declaration of Present State of Mind to Show Subsequent Conduct

A person's out-of-court declaration of state of mind when in issue may be admissible to prove the probability that the person engaged in some subsequent act pursuant to that declared state of mind.

Sue's testimony that her refusal to pay Jenks a bribe in exchange for her release on a prostitution arrest precipitated a threat from Jenks to "...get you and all your friends." Jenks' words demonstrate an out-of-court declaration of his own intended state of mind to seek revenge on Sue and her friends. Assuming Jenks' state of mind is at issue in relation to Tim's accusation of a frame up, such testimony may be admissible to prove the probability that Jenks' subsequent act of arresting Tim was done, not in the interests of legitimate police work, but pursuant to his declared state of mind to set Sue's friends up by framing Tim for heroin possession.

Sue's testimony may be admissible as a declaration of present state of mind to show subsequent conduct.

5) DR. WALT'S TESTIMONY RE: TIM'S PHYSICAL EXAMINATION

a) "Complaints of Insomnia/Anxiety"

Logical Relevancy

Defined supra.

On September 9, 1984 Dr. Walt examined Tim who complained of insomnia and anxiety. The prosecution will assert that these symptoms have a tendency in reason to prove that Tim was a heroin addict, a disputed fact of consequence to the determination of the felony possession action.

The testimony is logically relevant.

Hearsay

Defined supra.

Tim's complaints were made at Dr. Walt's office, outside the present proceeding. As such, they are an out-of-court statements. They are being offered to prove that Tim was a heroin user, the truth of the matter asserted.

Tim's statements are hearsay.

Exception - State of Body

Where a person's physical condition at a specified time is at issue, that person's spontaneous statements to a treating physician made at that time are admissible to prove the existence of the condition.

Tim's complaints were made during a medical examination to his treating physician, Dr. Walt. Because his complaints concerned addictive symptoms, his physical condition was at issue. The complaints appear to have been made spontaneously for purposes of diagnosis and treatment. They are admissible to prove the existence of his condition at that time.

The state of body exception is valid.

Physician-Patient Privilege

A patient has a privilege to refuse to disclose, and to prevent his physician from disclosing, any information relating to treatment obtained by the physician while treating the patient. The majority of jurisdictions hold that the physician-patient privilege cannot be invoked in a criminal proceeding.

Tim will assert that his complaints were made to Dr. Walt in confidence. They were made while Dr. Walt was conducting an examination for purposes of diagnosis and treatment during the doctor/patient relationship.

Since Tim is the patient and holder of the privilege, he has the right to prevent Dr. Walt from disclosing his complaints. However, because this case involves a criminal proceeding, i.e., State v. Tim, under the majority of jurisdictions, the privilege cannot be invoked.

Therefore, Tim's statements are not protected by the physician/patient privilege.

b) Tim's Statement, "I Am A Narcotics Addict In Need of Money"

Logical Relevancy

Defined supra.

Dr. Walt's testimony concerning Tim's statement that he was a narcotic addict and needed money to supply his habit has a tendency in reason to prove that Tim kept heroin on his person for personal use and sale, a disputed fact of consequence to the determination of the State's felony action against Tim for heroin possession.

Dr. Walt's testimony is logically relevant.

Hearsay

Defined and discussed supra.

Exception - Admission

A party to the litigation asserts a belief inconsistent with a position taken at trial.

Tim is the party defendant in the present action. His statement to Dr. Walt that he was a narcotics addict in need of money is a statement of his addiction which is inconsistent with his position at trial that he was not in possession of heroin for personal use and sale.

Tim's statement is admissible as a party admission.

Physician-Patient Privilege

Defined supra.

Tim made the statement to Dr. Walt in confidence during a medical examination. Although his admission to being a narcotics addict may be related to his diagnosis and treatment, his need for money to support that habit is not.

The portion of the statement concerning Tim's addiction will be protected by the privilege only in a minority of jurisdictions. However, the portion of the statement concerning Tim's need for money to support the habit is not privileged under any jurisdiction.

c) "Tim's Offer To Sell Dr. Drugs"

Logical Relevancy

Defined supra.

Tim's offer to sell Dr. Walt drugs on September 9, 1984 has a tendency in reason to prove that Tim had heroin in his possession for such purposes, a fact of consequence to the determination of the State's felony possession action against Tim.

Dr. Walt's testimony is logically relevant.

Hearsay

Defined supra.

Tim's statement is an out-of-court statement supra. It is being offered to prove that he was regularly in possession of drugs for purposes of personal use and sale, the truth of the matter asserted.

Tim's statement is hearsay.

Exception - Admission

Defined and discussed supra.

Physician-Patient Privilege

Defined supra.

Since Tim's offer to sell drugs was not related to Dr. Walt's diagnosis and treatment, it will not be protected by the privilege.

Legal Relevance

No evidence may be admitted where its probative value is substantially outweighed by its prejudicial impact.

Tim's statement is admitted to show his motive and readiness to carry heroin, not only to supply his own habit but to sell it to make money. This evidence would undoubtedly bias them into believing that if he was offering to sell narcotics to his own doctor, he must be selling to others as well. The probative value of this evidence is substantially outweighed by the prejudicial impact it would have on the jury.

The evidence should be excluded as legally irrelevant.

NOTE To Students Regarding Criminal Procedure Issues

The call of the question specifically requests whether items of evidence 1-5 were properly admitted. Therefore, while issues of arrest and search are raised in paragraph one, no discussion would be required for a passing grade.

EVIDENCE QUESTION #2

PAULA v. OWNER

Bob was struck by an automobile owned by Owner and driven by Chauf, Owner's employee. After two weeks in a hospital, Bob died. Chauf was convicted of involuntary vehicular manslaughter. He died in a prison knife fight one week after he was imprisoned.

Paula, Bob's wife, sued Owner for the wrongful death of Bob, alleging that Owner is liable, both on the doctrine of respondeat superior and because Owner was negligent in hiring Chauf. At the trial by jury, the following occurred:

(1) Paula's first witness, Carl, a police officer, testified: that when he arrived on the scene immediately after the accident, he asked Bob what had happened but he does not remember what Bob said; that, however, he had immediately made a note of what Bob told him and incorporated it in his written report. Carl verified the accuracy of his report and read it aloud. The report stated that Bob told Carl that he, Bob, was crossing the street when a speeding car crossed over the center line and hit him. Upon Paula's request, the report was introduced into evidence.

(2) Paula next called Dr. Flo, who testified: that she was on duty when Bob arrived at the hospital; that Bob complained of severe pain in his stomach and head; that Bob swore he would get even with the driver of the car that hit him; and that when asked what happened, Bob said he was hit by a speeding car driven by a drunken lunatic.

(3) Paula next called Earl, the warden of the prison where Chauf died, who identified a writing made by Chauf a few hours before Chauf's death. The writing commenced with the statement, "I believe I am about to die and I make this statement with no hope of recovery." The writing recited that Chauf was intoxicated and was driving about 80 mph in a 25 mph speed zone at the time of the accident. The writing was admitted into evidence.

(4) Paula next called Frank, who testified: that he had known Bob for thirty years, that he had seen Bob on many occasions cross the intersection where the accident occurred; and that Bob always waited for the green light and looked both ways before crossing the street.

(5) Paula called Owner as an adverse witness and asked Owner whether he had heard that Chauf had received five traffic citations over the last five years for driving under the influence of alcohol. Owner asked: "No, because Chauf never had a traffic citation."

Assume all appropriate objections were timely made. Were the items of evidence (1) through (4) properly admitted and was the question and answer in item (5) proper? Discuss.

IRAC OUTLINE SHEET

(I)	(R)	(A)	(C)

EXAMPLE OF PROPER IRAC OUTLINE

PAULA v. OWNER

(1) **TESTIMONY OF CARL (C)**

(I)	(R)	(A)	(C)
LOGICAL RELEVANCY	Tendency In Reason To Prove/Disprove Disputed Fact	P's first witness, C, a police officer testified he arrived on scene/made a note of what B told him/report stated B told C that B was crossing street when speeding car crossed over center line & hit him	Logically Relevant
	Consequence To Action	B's truck by auto owned by O/driven by Chauf O's employee/P, B's wife, sued O for wrongful death of B/alleged O liable on doctrine of respondeat superior/negligent hiring of Chauf	
LAY OPINION	Common Law-Prohibited Modern Law-Admissible		Valid Lay Opinion
	Personal Observations/Facts In Dispute	B hit by speeding car	
	No Better Evidence	Speeding car	
HEARSAY	Out-Of-Court Statement	C arrived on scene/asked B what happened C made a note of what B told him & incorporated it in his written report B crossing street when speeding car crossed center line/hit him	Hearsay
	Offered For Truth Of Matter Asserted	Wrongful death/respondeat superior/negligent hiring	
MULTIPLE HEARSAY	Extrajudicial Words Incorporating/Repeating Other Hearsay	C made a note of what B told him/incorporated it in his written report	Multiple Hearsay
EXCEPTION-PAST RECOLLECTION RECORDED	No Recollection When Testifying	When C arrived on scene asked B what happened but doesn't remember what B said	Valid Exception
	Writing Prepared By Witness/Personal Knowledge	C immediately made note of what B told him/incorporated it in his written report	
	Matter Fresh In Memory When Reported	C immediately made note of what B told him/incorporated it in his written report	
	Witness Vouches Accuracy	C verified accuracy of his report	
EXCEPTION-EXCITED UTTERANCE	Exciting Event	B crossing street/speeding car crossover center line/hit him	Valid Exception
	Stimulus/Spontaneous Statement	C arrived on scene immediately after accident/asked B what happened/B told C speeding car hit him supra	
	Relates To Cause Of Excitement	B told C speeding car hit him supra	
	Personal Knowledge	B struck by auto	
PRESENT SENSE IMPRESSION	Statement Contemporaneous With Event While Perceiving It	Immediately after accident, C asked B what happened	Valid Exception
	Statement Describes Event	B told C was crossing street/speeding car crossed center line/hit him supra	

(2) **TESTIMONY OF DR. FLO (F)**

a) **Complaints Of Severe Stomach/Head Pain**

(I)	(R)	(A)	(C)
LOGICAL RELEVANCY	Tendency In Reason To Prove/Disprove Disputed Fact	F on duty when B arrived at hospital/B complained of severe pain in his stomach & head	Logically Relevant
	Consequence To Action	Wrongful death	
HEARSAY	Out-Of-Court Statement	B arrived at hospital/complained supra	Hearsay
	Offered For Truth Of Matter Asserted	Severe pain/wrongful death	
EXCEPTION-STATE OF BODY	Physical Condition At Issue	B complained of severe pain in stomach/head from accident	Valid Exception
	Spontaneous Statement To Treating Physician	Dr. F on duty when B arrived at hospital	
	Prove Existence Of Condition	Injuries from accident	

b) B Swore He Would Get Even With Driver

(I)	(R)	(A)	(C)
LOGICAL RELEVANCY	Tendency In Reason To Prove/Disprove Disputed Fact Consequence To Action	B swore he would get even with driver that hit him Wrongful death action (victim of speeding driver?)	Logically Relevant
HEARSAY	Out-Of-Court Statement Offered For Truth Of Matter Asserted	B arrived at hospital/swore to get even Driver of the car hit him	Hearsay
EXCEPTION-EXCITED UTTERANCE	Exciting Event	B hit/B arrived at hospital/severe pain/swore	Valid Exception
	Stimulus/Spontaneous Statement Relates To Cause Of Excitement Personal Knowledge	B swore supra B swore supra B was hit	

c) B Said Speeding Car/Drunken Lunatic

(I)	(R)	(A)	(C)
LOGICAL RELEVANCY	Tendency In Reason To Prove/Disprove Disputed Fact Consequence To Action	B said he was hit by speeding car driven by drunken lunatic Wrongful death	Logically Relevant
LAY OPINION	Common Law-Prohibited Modern Law-Admissible Personal Observations/Facts In Dispute No Better Evidence	 Speeding car driven by drunken lunatic Speeding/drunken lunatic	Arguable
HEARSAY	Out-Of-Court Statement Offered For Truth Of Matter Asserted	B arrived at hospital/said he was hit supra B said he was hit supra	Hearsay
EXCEPTION-EXCITED UTTERANCE	Exciting Event	B said hit by car/drunken lunatic supra	
	Stimulus/Spontaneous Statement Relates To Cause Of Excitement Personal Knowledge	? B said he was hit supra Drunken lunatic	
PRESENT SENSE IMPRESSION	Statement Contemporaneous With Event While Perceiving It Statement Describes Event	B arrived at hospital/said hit supra Drunken lunatic	Invalid Exception

(3) EARL'S (E) TESTIMONY IDENTIFYING CHAUF'S WRITING

(I)	(R)	(A)	(C)
LOGICAL RELEVANCY	Tendency In Reason To Prove/Disprove Disputed Fact	E identified writing made by Chauf/recited that Chauf intoxicated/driving 80 mph in 25 mph zone at time of accident P alleges O liable as respondeat superior for negligent hiring	Logically Relevant
	Consequence To Action	Auto owned by O/driven by Chauf, O's employee	
AUTHENTICATION	Lay Witness Personal Knowledge Opinion Verify Handwriting	E, warden E, warden of prison where Chauf died Warden identified writing made by Chauf supra	Authenticated
HEARSAY	Out-Of-Court Statement Offered For Truth Of Matter Asserted	Writing made by Chauf a few hours before his death Chauf intoxicated/driving 80 mph supra	Hearsay
EXCEPTION-VICARIOUS ADMISSION	Admission By 3rd Party	C, O's employee admitted	
	Independent Existence Of Agency Proven Facts Related To Current Matters	Auto driven by Chauf, O' s employee Writing recited that Chauf intoxicated/driving 80 mph supra P sued O supra	Arguable
	Statement Made Within Scope Of Agent's Authority/Employment	Statement made in prison referred to driving while employed by O?	
EXCEPTION-DECLARATION AGAINST INTEREST	Declarant A Non-Party To Litigation	P sued O for wrongful death	Invalid Exception
	Declarant Unavailable To Testify	Chauf died in prison one week after he was imprisoned	
	Personal Knowledge	Chauf's writing/intoxicated/driving 80 mph supra	
	Against Declarant's Interest	"I believe I am about to die"	

(I)	(R)	(A)	(C)
EXCEPTION-DYING DECLARATION	Declarant Unavailable	Chauf died in prison	Invalid Exception
	Believes Death Imminent	I believe I am about to die/I make statement with no hope of recovery	
	Relates To Cause Of Death	He died in a prison knife fight	
	Personal Knowledge	Knife fight	
(4) TESTIMONY OF FRANK			
LOGICAL RELEVANCY	Tendency In Reason To Prove/Disprove Disputed Fact	Known B For 30 years/seen B on many occasions cross intersection/B always waited for green before crossing	Logically Relevant
	Consequence To Action	Wrongful death	
CHARACTER EVIDENCE	Acting In Conformity With Character	Knew for 30 years/seen B on many occasions cross intersection/always waited, looked supra (civil case?)	Improper Character
HABIT EVIDENCE	Routine Response Frequently Repeated	Seen B on many occasions cross intersection/always waited looked supra	Proper Habit
	Protracted Period Of Time	30 years/many occasions	
(5) OWNER'S TESTIMONY			
LOGICAL RELEVANCY	Tendency In Reason To Prove/Disprove Disputed Fact	Whether O had heard that Chauf received 5 traffic citations over last 5 years for DUI	Logically Relevant
	Consequence To Action	Negligent hiring	
CHARACTER EVIDENCE	Acting In Conformity With Character	Chauf received 5 traffic tickets over last 5 years for DUI/intoxicated and driving 80 mph in 25 mph zone at time of accident (civil action)	Improper Character
LIMITED ADMISSIBILITY	Evidence Inadmissible For One Purpose May Be Admissible For Another	5 traffic tickets over past 5 years for DUI (civil case?) Negligent hiring (notice)	Limited admissibility
LEGAL RELEVANCE	Probative v. Prejudicial	Chauf's past driving record for DUI's (act in conformity with past record?)	Arguable
NON RESPONSIVE ANSWER	Answer Non-Responsive To Question	Have you heard that Chauf had received supra No, because Chauf never had a traffic citation	Non Responsive Answer

EXAMPLE OF IRAC EVIDENCE ISSUE

(I) **Exception to Bob's Statement - Excited Utterance**

(R) The statement of any person made (1) at the time of some exciting event and under the stimulus of his excitement may be admissible if it is (2) spontaneous, (3) relates to the cause of the excitement and is (4) within the personal knowledge of that person.

(A) When Bob was hit by a speeding car that crossed over the center line while he was crossing the street, the incident created a shocking and (1) exciting event. Carl arrived on the scene immediately after the accident and asked Bob what happened. Bob told Carl that he had been hit by a speeding car, a (2) spontaneous statement in response to Carl's question while Bob was still under the stimulus of the accident. His statement (3) related to the cause of the accident. Since he was the victim of the automobile accident, the circumstances of the accident were (4) within his personal knowledge.

(C) Excited utterance is a valid exception.

SUGGESTED MODEL ANSWER

PAULA v. OWNER - WRONGFUL DEATH

(1) TESTIMONY OF CARL: BOB'S STATEMENT CONTAINED IN HIS WRITTEN REPORT

Logical Relevance

Evidence is logically relevant if it has any tendency in reason to prove or disprove a disputed fact of consequence to the determination of the action.

Carl testified that when he arrived at the scene of the accident, he made a note of what Bob told him. His police report documented Bob's statement to Carl that as he was crossing the street, a speeding car crossed over the center line and hit him. This information has a tendency in reason to prove that Bob was hit by a car driven by Chauf, Owner's employee. Such a disputed fact is of consequence to the determination of Owner's liability under respondeat superior arising from his negligent hiring alleged in Paula's wrongful death action.

Therefore, the testimony is logically relevant.

Lay Opinion

Common law prohibited lay opinion. Modernly, lay opinion will be admissible when it is a result of that witness' personal observation of facts in dispute and when no better evidence can be reasonably obtained.

Bob stated that he was hit by a speeding car. Under common law, Bob's opinion that the car was speeding was prohibited.

Modernly, lay persons can reasonably perceive a measurement of speed from past experience and can form an accurate opinion. Such a statement would be helpful to a judge or jury when determining whether the driver was negligent. It appears that no better evidence can be obtained to dispute his observations.

Bob's lay opinion is admissible.

Hearsay

Hearsay is an out-of-court statement offered to prove the truth of the matter asserted.

Carl testified that when he arrived on the scene and asked Bob what happened, Bob told him that while he was crossing the street, a speeding car crossed the line and hit him. Bob's statement was incorporated into Carl's written report, outside of the present proceeding. Therefore, it was an out-of-court statement.

Carl's testimony is being offered to prove that the driver of the car was negligent. If Chauf is identified as the driver and is shown to be Owner's employee, his negligence can be imputed to Owner under respondeat superior, the truth of the matter asserted.

The testimony is inadmissible hearsay.

Multiple Hearsay

Multiple hearsay is extra-judicial words or conduct which repeat or incorporate other hearsay. Such is admissible only where each part of the statement or conduct falls within one of the exceptions to the hearsay rule.

Carl made a note of what Bob told him and incorporated it into his written report at the scene of the accident, outside-of-court. It is being offered for the truth of its contents making it a hearsay statement. Carl's note documenting what Bob told him contains extra-judicial words incorporated in that report and is also considered hearsay.

Therefore, each hearsay statement must fall within a recognized exception to be admissible.

Exception as to the Report - Past Recollection Recorded

Where a witness has no recollection at the time of testifying to testify fully and accurately to the facts contained in a writing, that writing is admissible if it was prepared by the witness within his personal knowledge, the matter was fresh in the witness' memory when recorded, and he vouches for its accuracy.

Carl testified that when he arrived on the scene of the accident, he asked Bob what happened. He does not remember what Bob said demonstrating his insufficient recollection for purposes of testimony. Carl immediately made a note of what Bob told him satisfying the requirement for a writing prepared by the witness within his personal knowledge. Carl immediately made a note of what Bob told him and incorporated it into his written report while the matter was still fresh in his memory. Carl verified the accuracy of his report. Since he now has no recollection of what he wrote, the report itself is admissible.

Past recollection recorded is a valid exception.

Exception to Bob's Statement - Excited Utterance

The statement of any person made at the time of some exciting event and under the stimulus of his excitement may be admissible if it is spontaneous, relates to the cause of the excitement and is within the personal knowledge of that person.

When Bob was hit by a speeding car that crossed over the center line while he was crossing the street, the incident created a shocking and exciting event. Carl arrived on the scene immediately after the accident and asked Bob what happened. Bob told Carl that he had been hit by a speeding car, a spontaneous statement in response to Carl's question while Bob was still under the stimulus of the accident. His statement related to the cause of the accident. Since he was the victim of the automobile accident, the circumstances of the accident were within his personal knowledge.

Excited utterance is a valid exception.

Exception - Present Sense Impression

The federal rules permit admission of a statement made by a person contemporaneous with the event while perceiving it and which describes or explains that event or condition.

Bob's statement was made immediately after being hit while crossing the street. Even though it was not contemporaneous with the event of being hit, it was made in response to Carl's question and so soon after the accident that it would be within the time that Bob was perceiving himself the victim of a speeding driver. Bob was describing his actions and those of the speeding driver which resulted in his being hit.

Present sense impression is a valid exception. Therefore, Carl's report and Bob's statements contained therein will be admissible.

(2) TESTIMONY OF DR. FLO: BOB'S STATEMENTS IN HOSPITAL

a. Complaints of Severe Stomach/Head Pain

Logical Relevance

Defined supra.

Dr. Flo testified that she was on duty when Bob arrived at the hospital. At that time, he complained of severe pain in his stomach and head. Bob's complaints have a tendency in reason to prove that he had been hit and seriously injured by a speeding driver, a disputed fact of consequence to the determination of the wrongful death action.

The testimony is logically relevant.

Hearsay

Defined supra.

Bob's statement was made when he arrived at the hospital and is an out-of-court statement. It is offered to prove that he was suffering from severe pain in his stomach and head that ultimately caused his wrongful death, the truth of the matter asserted.

The testimony is inadmissible hearsay.

Exception - State of Body

Where a person's physical condition at a specified time is at issue, that person's spontaneous statements made to a treating physician are admissible to prove the existence of the condition.

Bob's complaints concerning the severe pain related to his stomach and head pain resulting from the accident were vital to his treatment at the specified time when he arrived at the hospital. Further, because his complaints related directly to the injuries sustained in the accident, his physical condition is at issue. Bob's statement concerned how he felt and appear to have been spontaneously made to Dr. Flo, his treating physician, as a result of the pain that he was experiencing from his injuries. His complaints prove the existence of his compromised physical condition at that time.

State of body is a valid exception.

b. "Get Even With the Driver that Hit Me"

Logical Relevance

Defined supra.

Bob's sworn threat to get even with the driver that hit him has a tendency in reason to prove that Bob was the victim of a speeding driver, a disputed fact of consequence to the determination of Paula's wrongful death action.

The testimony is logically relevant.

Hearsay

Defined supra.

Bob's sworn threat was made at the hospital, outside the present proceeding. As such, it is an out-of-court statement. It is offered to prove he was hit by a speeding driver, the truth of the matter asserted.

Bob's statement is inadmissible hearsay.

Exception - Excited Utterance

Defined supra.

Bob had been hit by a car. He arrived at the hospital suffering from stomach and head pain caused by his injuries at which time he was still under the stimulus of that shocking and exciting event. His threat to get even was a spontaneous statement made to Dr. Flo when he arrived at the hospital. It related to the speeding driver who was the cause of his excitement. Since he was the victim, he had personal knowledge of the accident.
Excited utterance is a valid exception.

c. "Speeding Car/Drunken Lunatic"

Logical Relevance

Defined supra.

Bob's statement that he was hit by a speeding car driven by a drunken lunatic has a tendency in reason to prove that driver was negligent, a disputed fact of consequence to the determination of Owner's liability as alleged in Paula's wrongful death action.

The testimony is logically relevant.

Lay Opinion

Defined supra.

Bob was estimating that the driver was speeding. At common law, Bob's opinion that the car was speeding was prohibited. Modernly, as discussed previously, this is an assessment that can be made by a lay person. Such a statement would be helpful to a judge or jury when determining whether the driver was negligent. It appears that no better evidence can be obtained to dispute his opinion. Therefore, Bob's testimony concerning the speed of the car is a valid lay opinion.

However, his statement that the driver was a drunken lunatic is a legal conclusion concerning intoxication and insanity. This determination is not a measurement that can be assessed without the expertise of an expert with specialized knowledge.

Therefore, the portion of the statement relating to the speed may be admissible, but the portion of the statement regarding the drunken lunatic must be severed as inadmissible.

Hearsay

Defined and discussed supra under 2a. and b.

Exception - Excited Utterance

Defined supra.

Bob made the above-mentioned statement in the hospital after the accident, a shocking and exciting event. Although he may have still been under the stimulus of the accident and the statement related to the cause of the accident, it may not have been spontaneous. There is no indication that Bob had personal knowledge of the driver's drunkenness or whether the driver was a lunatic.

Therefore, excited utterance will not apply.

Exception - Present Sense Impression

Defined supra.

Bob's threats were made when Bob arrived at the hospital. Since he arrived there soon after the accident, it may be considered contemporaneous with the event from which he was perceiving himself as an accident victim. Bob was describing the driver and the driver's actions which resulted in the accident. However, he had no way of knowing that the driver was either drunk or a lunatic. Thus, his description of the driver was not valid.

Present sense impression is not a valid exception.

(3) TESTIMONY OF EARL AS TO A WRITING HE IDENTIFIED AS CHAUF'S

Logical Relevance

Defined supra.

Earl identified a writing made by Chauf that recited that Chauf was intoxicated and driving 80 mph in a 25 mph zone at the time of the accident. This testimony has a tendency in reason to prove that Chauf was driving Owner's car, a disputed fact of consequence to the determination of Owner's liability under respondeat superior as alleged in Paula's wrongful death action.

The testimony is logically relevant.

Authentication - Handwriting

A lay witness who has personal knowledge of the handwriting of another may state his opinion as to its authenticity.

Earl was a lay witness. As the prison warden where Chauf died, he may have had personal knowledge of Chauf's handwriting. Earl identified Chauf's written confession as having been made by Chauf. Since Earl was the warden of the prison where Chauf died, he would be in a position to identify Chauf's handwriting if he had witnessed it on other documents signed by Chauf when Chauf was originally imprisoned. Since Earl is stating his opinion as to its authenticity, it appears his testimony would be sufficient to verify Chauf's handwritten confession.

The document has been properly authenticated.

Hearsay

Defined supra.

Chauf's writing was made a few hours before he died in prison, outside the present proceeding. As such, it is an out-of-court statement. It is being offered to prove that Chauf was intoxicated and speeding at the time he hit Bob, the truth of the matter asserted.

The testimony is inadmissible hearsay.

Exception - Vicarious Admission

Admissions made by a third party may be imputed to another party and may be admissible against that party if independent existence of the agency is proven, the facts relate to the current matters, and the statement was made within the scope of the agent's authority or employment.

Chauf was Owner's employee but not a defendant in the Paula v. Owner lawsuit. He would be considered a third party to that action. The prosecution must prove that Owner hired Chauf by independent evidence of his employment, i.e., paychecks, W-2's, etc. The confession stated that Chauf was drunk and speeding 80 mph in a 25 mph zone when he hit Bob. These facts relate to the current trial matter concerning Chauf's negligence and Owner's liability under respondeat superior. The accident took place while Chauf was ostensibly driving Owner's car during the scope of his employment.

Owner will argue that he did not authorize Chauf to make any statements concerning his employment. Further, the statement was made while Chauf was in prison and not within the scope of his employment.

Under common law, vicarious admissions were limited to those relating to the nature of the employment. Since the cause of the accident was not directly related to Chauf's contract to drive for Owner, it would not be an admission chargeable against Owner.

However, the evidentiary value of such statements is overwhelming. The federal rules would admit them against Owner since they concerned matters within the scope of Chauf's employment and there are no facts that the employment had been terminated at the time Chauf wrote the confession.

Therefore, vicarious admission is a valid exception.

Exception - Declaration Against Interest

A statement may be received into evidence if the person who made the statement is not a party to the action, is unavailable to testify, the statement was within the person's personal knowledge at the time, and the statement was made against an important interest of the declarant.

Chauf made the statement concerning his drunken condition when he hit Bob. Since Paula sued Owner only, Chauf was not a party to the Paula/Owner lawsuit. His death in prison made him unavailable to testify at trial. Chauf's intoxication and speeding were matters within his personal knowledge. However, since he was dying when he made his statements, these statements did not create an important immediate and substantial prejudice to his financial or proprietary interests.

Declaration against interest is an invalid exception.

Exception - Dying Declaration

Statements of a victim regarding the cause or circumstances of his impending death are admissible if the declarant is unavailable, believed that death was imminent when making the statement, the statement relates to the cause of death and is within the declarant's personal knowledge.

Chauf died in prison, the victim of a prison knife fight, making him unavailable to testify at the time of trial. A few hours before his death, Chauf wrote "I believe I am about to die and I make this statement with no hope of recovery." Such facts demonstrate that Chauf believed that death was imminent. However, he stated that he was intoxicated and was driving 80 mph in a 25 mph zone at the time of the accident. This statement does not relate to the cause of his death from the knife fight even though it was within his personal knowledge.

Dying declaration is an invalid exception.

(4) TESTIMONY OF FRANK AS TO BOB'S CONDUCT

Logical Relevance

Defined supra.

Frank's testimony that he had known Bob for thirty years . . .and that Bob always waited for the green light . . . had a tendency in reason to prove the disputed fact that Bob was legally crossing the street when he was hit. This fact is of consequence to the determination that Chauf, not Bob, caused the accident in the wrongful death action.

The testimony is logically relevant.

Character Evidence

Evidence of some trait of a person's character may be offered to prove that the person was likely to have acted in conformity with that character.

Frank's testimony that he had seen Bob cross the intersection on many occasions and he'd always waited for the green light and looked both ways before crossing is being offered to prove that since Bob always acted with care when crossing a street, he was likely to have acted in conformity with that trait on the day he was struck by Chauf. Since Frank knew Bob personally for 30 years, he would be permitted to give his opinion as to Bob's probable conduct.

However, in a civil case such as this one, Paula v. Owner for wrongful death, character evidence of this nature is generally inadmissible.

Frank's testimony is improper character evidence.

Habit Evidence

Habit evidence is admissible if a particular activity, routine or response is frequently repeated over a protracted period of time.

Frank testified that he had seen Bob cross the intersection in question on many occasions. Bob always waited for the green light and looked both ways before crossing. His routine before crossing was frequently repeated on every occasion that Frank observed. Further, Frank knew Bob for thirty years and observed this behavior over that protracted period of time.

Therefore, it is likely that Bob acted in accordance with this habit on the day that he was struck by Chauf.

Frank's habit testimony is admissible.

(5) TESTIMONY OF OWNER AS TO CHAUF'S PRIOR DRIVING RECORD

Logical Relevance

Defined supra.

Whether Owner had heard that Chauf had received five traffic citations over the last five years for drunk driving has a tendency in reason to prove that Chauf had a five year history of drunk driving that Owner should have been aware of before he hired him. This is a disputed fact of consequence to the determination of whether Owner negligently hired Chauf to drive Owner's car making him liable under respondeat superior for the wrongful death action.

The question is logically relevant.

Character Evidence

Defined supra.

Evidence that Chauf had received five traffic citations over the last five years for driving under the influence of alcohol is being offered to prove that Chauf was likely to have acted in conformity with his tendency to drive in a drunken state when he hit Bob.

However, since this is a civil case, character evidence is generally inadmissible to reflect on whether Chauf acted in a particular way on this occasion.

Paul's question is inadmissible character evidence.

Limited Admissibility

Evidence that is inadmissible for one purpose, it is not necessarily inadmissible for another purpose and may be offered for purposes other than to show probable conduct.

Even though the question of Chauf's record showing a five year history of driving under the influence is inadmissible character evidence in this civil case, it is proper to show that Owner should have been on notice of Chauf's past driving record. Such notice would prove Paula's negligent hiring allegation, not probable conduct.

The question will be allowed under the doctrine of limited admissibility.

Legal Relevance

No evidence may be admitted where its probative value is substantially outweighed by its prejudicial impact.

Owner will argue that the evidence of Chauf's past driving record will mislead the jury into believing that since Chauf drove drunk on five known prior occasions, he surely acted in conformity with his past record on the occasion in question. The prejudicial impact of such evidence substantially outweighs the probative value of any notice arguments.

It is arguable as to whether the court will exclude this evidence.

Non-responsive Answer

Answers given by a witness must be in direct response to the question asked.

Owner's answer, "No, because Chauf never had a traffic citation" was not in direct response to the question asked as to whether he had heard that Chauf had received five traffic citations . . . for driving under the influence of alcohol.

The answer after "No," should be struck as a non responsive answer.

NOTE TO STUDENT

Due to the length and complexity of this exam, the student analysis under exam conditions may be more conclusary than shown in this model answer.

EVIDENCE QUESTION #3

STATE v. DICK

Dick is brought to trial on an indictment charging him with larceny of a dangerous drug, a statutory offense. The prosecution's theory of the case, as revealed by its opening statement, is that Phil saw Dick enter Phil's Pharmacy, loiter about the prescription counter, reach behind the counter, grab two bottles, and flee by car. Phil called police officers who arrested Dick after a lengthy high speed chase.

At the trial before a jury, the following events occur:

(a) The prosecution offers in evidence a properly authenticated transcript of testimony by Officer Oats given during a previous trial of Dick for reckless driving based on the high speed chase from Phil's Pharmacy. Oats' testimony was that during the chase and while Dick's car was passing over a bridge, two objects were ejected from Dick's car window and into the river below. It is stipulated that Dick was represented by counsel at the earlier trial and that Oats is now deceased.

(b) The prosecution offers the testimony of Phil that the bottles seized by Dick were labeled "DLD," that the bottles were the original labeled containers received from the supplier, and that the bottles had not been opened.

(c) The prosecution requests the court to take judicial notice that "DLD" is a derivative of opium. The statute under which Dick is prosecuted does not list "DLD" as a "dangerous drug," but does define dangerous drugs to include "any derivative of opium." In support of its request the prosecution offers for the court's inspection a standard pharmacological dictionary, which defines "DLD" as an opium derivative.

(d) The prosecution offers the testimony of Dick's divorced wife, Win, that during her marriage to Dick the latter frequently used narcotics but attempted to conceal the fact from Win.

Assume all appropriate objections are made by Dick.

How should the court rule on each of the prosecution's offers and requests? Discuss.

IRAC OUTLINE SHEET

(I)	(R)	(A)	(C)

EXAMPLE OF PROPER IRAC OUTLINE

STATE (S) v. DICK (D)

(a) TRANSCRIPT OF OFFICER OATS' TESTIMONY (O)

(I)	(R)	(A)	(C)
LOGICAL RELEVANCY	Tendency In Reason To Prove/Disprove Disputed Fact	Transcript of O's testimony given during a previous trial of D for reckless driving based on the high speed chase from P's pharmacy	Logically Relevant
	Consequence To Action	D brought to trial on indictment charging him with larceny of a dangerous drug	
HEARSAY	Out-Of-Court Statement	Transcript of testimony by O given during a previous trial of D supra	
	Offered For Truth Of Matter Asserted	D charged with larceny High speed chase from pharmacy Two objects ejected from D's car supra	Hearsay
EXCEPTION-PRIOR REPORTED TESTIMONY	Oath/Opportunity To Cross-Examine	It is stipulated that D was represented by counsel at the earlier trial	
	Identity Of Parties	State/Dick	Valid Exception
	Identity Of Issues	Previous trial for reckless driving D is brought to trial for larceny of a dangerous drug	
	Declarant Unavailable	O is now deceased	

(b) TESTIMONY OF PHIL (P)

(I)	(R)	(A)	(C)
LOGICAL RELEVANCY	Tendency In Reason To Prove/Disprove Disputed Fact	Testimony of P that bottles seized by D were labeled DLD	Logically Relevant
	Consequence To Action	Indictment charging D with larceny of a dangerous drug	
AUTHENTICATION	Proponent Must Present Evidence Of Chain Of Custody	Bottles seized by D were labeled DLD/ the bottles were the original labeled containers received from the supplier/bottles had not been opened	Authenticated
BEST EVIDENCE RULE	Content Of A Writing	Bottles seized by D labeled DLD	
	Original Must Be Produced Unless Unavailable	Two objects ejected from D's car window into river below supra	Inapplicable
SECONDARY EVIDENCE	Majority-Copy Required Federal/Minority-No Preference	Copy of label available? P's testimony	Admissible
HEARSAY	Out-Of-Court Statement	Bottles labeled DLD/original labeled containers received from supplier	Hearsay
	Offered For Truth Of Matter Asserted	D charged with larceny of dangerous drug, a statutory offense	
EXCEPTION-FEDERAL RULE CATCHALL	Trustworthy	P's pharmacy?	
	Material Fact/Probative Notice To Opponent	D charged with drug larceny supra ?	Valid Exception

(c) PROSECUTION'S REQUEST FOR JUDICIAL NOTICE

(I)	(R)	(A)	(C)
LOGICAL RELEVANCY	Tendency In Reason To Prove/Disprove Disputed Fact	DLD a derivative of opium	Logically Relevant
	Consequence To Action	Statute under which D prosecuted does not list DLD as a dangerous drug but defines dangerous drugs to include any derivative of opium	
JUDICIAL NOTICE (Permissive)	Court Accepts Facts Not Subject To Dispute	Prosecution requests court to take judicial notice that DLD is a derivative of opium/statute	No Judicial Notice
	No Necessity For Formal Proof	Statute under which D prosecuted does not list DLD as dangerous drug supra Prosecution offers for court's inspection a standard pharmacological dictionary which defines DLD as opium derivative (element of a crime?)	

(I)	(R)	(A)	(C)
(d) **<u>TESTIMONY OF WIN (W)</u>**			
<u>LOGICAL RELEVANCY</u>	Tendency In Reason To Prove/Disprove Disputed Fact	Testimony of W that during her marriage to D, D frequently used narcotics but attempted to conceal that fact from W	Logically Relevant
	Consequence To Action	D charged with larceny dangerous drug	
<u>SPOUSAL TESTIMONIAL PRIVILEGE</u>	Marital Relationship	Testimony of D's divorced wife, W	No Privilege
	Privilege Not To Testify	Ø	
<u>SPOUSAL COMMUNICATION PRIVILEGE</u>	Confidential Communications During Marriage	During W's marriage to D, D frequently used narcotics but attempted to conceal the fact from W (non-verbal communication/ observation?)	Arguable

EXAMPLE OF IRAC EVIDENCE ISSUE

(I) **Exception - Prior Reported Testimony (Former Testimony)**

(R) Under the majority rule, a transcript of a witness' testimony in a prior trial is admissible in the present proceeding if (1) there was an oath and opportunity to cross-examine during the prior proceeding, (2) sufficient identity of parties, (3) sufficient identity of issues, and (4) the declarant is unavailable for the present proceeding.

(A) The facts stipulate that Dick was represented by counsel at his earlier trial for reckless driving. Officer Oats' testimony was taken (1) under oath, giving Dick's counsel the motive and opportunity to carefully cross-examine him for inconsistencies in his testimony.

In both trials, the State was prosecuting Dick on criminal charges sufficient to demonstrate (2) identity of parties.

Dick will contend that the previous trial was for reckless driving. The second trial is for larceny of a dangerous drug. Since the elements that must be proven for a conviction on each count are not identical, under common law, (3) identity of issues would fail.

However, the reckless driving charge resulted from a high speed chase from the Pharmacy. This getaway was based upon the same set of circumstances from which the larceny indictment arose. Since the two events are closely related, modern law would hold them substantially similar sufficient to meet the identity of issues requirement.

Further, Officer Oats is now deceased demonstrating his (4) unavailability to testify at the present trial.

(C) In the majority of jurisdictions, the transcript of Officer Oats' testimony will be admissible under the prior reported testimony exception.

SUGGESTED MODEL ANSWER

STATE v. DICK

(a) TRANSCRIPT OF OFFICER OATS' TESTIMONY GIVEN DURING DICK'S PREVIOUS TRIAL

Logical Relevance

Evidence is logically relevant if it has any tendency in reason to prove or disprove a disputed fact of consequence to the determination of the action.

The introduction of the transcript containing Officer Oats' testimony given during Dick's previous trial for reckless driving trial based on the high speed chase from Phil's Pharmacy has a tendency in reason to prove that Dick stole drugs from that location, a disputed fact of consequence to the determination of the present action charging him with larceny of a dangerous drug.

Therefore, Oats' transcript is logically relevant.

Hearsay

Hearsay is an out-of-court statement offered to prove the truth of the matter asserted.

Since the transcript containing Officer Oats' testimony was produced at Dick's previous reckless driving trial, outside the present proceeding, it is an out-of-court statement.

Dick is charged with larceny. The prosecution is using Officer Oats' testimony to prove that Dick was involved in a high speed chase from the Pharmacy during which time he ejected two objects from his car. Since these objects were the tangible evidence of the alleged larceny of drugs, the prosecution is offering the transcript to prove that Dick committed the larceny, the truth of the matter asserted. The testimony is inadmissible hearsay under the majority rule.

However, under a minority of jurisdictions (**Wigmore**), prior reported testimony given under oath in a prior trial is considered admissible non-hearsay. It was subject to cross-examination sufficient to imply the trustworthiness of the testimony.

Exception - Prior Reported Testimony (Former Testimony)

Under the majority rule, a transcript of a witness' testimony in a prior trial is admissible in the present proceeding if there was an oath and opportunity to cross-examine during the prior proceeding, sufficient identity of parties, sufficient identity of issues, and the declarant is unavailable for the present proceeding.

The facts stipulate that Dick was represented by counsel at his earlier trial for reckless driving. Officer Oats' testimony was taken under oath, giving Dick's counsel the motive and opportunity to carefully cross-examine him for inconsistencies in his testimony.

In both trials, the State was prosecuting Dick on criminal charges sufficient to demonstrate identity of parties.

Dick will contend that the previous trial was for reckless driving. The second trial is for larceny of a dangerous drug. Since the elements that must be proven for a conviction on each count are not identical, under common law, identity of issues would fail.

However, the reckless driving charge resulted from a high speed chase from the Pharmacy. This getaway was based upon the same set of circumstances from which the larceny indictment arose. Since the two events are closely related, modern law would hold them substantially similar sufficient to meet the identity of issues requirement.

Further, Officer Oats is now deceased demonstrating his unavailability to testify at the present trial.

In the majority of jurisdictions, the transcript of Officer Oats' testimony will be admissible under the prior reported testimony exception.

(b) TESTIMONY OF PHIL - LABELS ON THE BOTTLES LABELED "DLD"

Logical Relevance

Defined supra.

Phil testified that the bottles seized by Dick were labeled DLD. Such testimony has a tendency in reason to prove that the bottles stolen from the Pharmacy contained a dangerous drug, a disputed fact of consequence to the determination of the larceny of a dangerous drug action.

The testimony is logically relevant.

Authentication - Chain of Custody

Where real evidence that is not of the type easily recognized, or is capable of causing confusion or subject to tampering, the proponent of the object must present evidence of its chain of custody.

Phil testified that the bottles allegedly seized from Phil's Pharmacy were labeled DLD. Such testimony is being used to identify the contents of the bottles as dangerous drugs. Since neither the bottles nor their contents have been introduced into evidence, Phil's testimony is not the type that a court could easily recognize as proof that the bottles did, in fact, contain this dangerous substance.

However, Phil's further testimony that the bottles in question were the original labeled containers received from the supplier and had not been opened raises the strong probability that substitution of the bottle contents or tampering with the bottles themselves had not occurred.

Phil's testimony reasonably indicates that the bottle labels correctly identified the bottle contents as DLD. The chain of custody from supplier to Pharmacy lends support to such identification.

Phil's testimony has been properly authenticated.

Best Evidence Rule

In order to prove the contents of a writing, the original must be produced unless it is unavailable.

Phil testified that the printed labels affixed to the bottles identified the substance contained in the bottles as DLD. Since he is testifying to the contents of a written label, the original labels must be produced.

However, during the high speed chase from the Pharmacy, Dick ejected the bottles with their attached labels out of his car window into the river. The labels were lost as a result of Dick's own conduct. Because the loss was without the fault of the declarant, the original labels do not have to be produced.

The best evidence rule will not apply.

Secondary Evidence

Where the best evidence rule is not applicable, the majority and California jurisdictions prefer a copy of the original writing if available. The federal and minority view will accept any kind of secondary evidence including oral testimony.

The prosecution is offering Phil's oral testimony to identify the contents of the bottle labels. Since the original labels have been lost and no copies appear available, under all jurisdictions, Phil's oral testimony will be admissible as secondary evidence.

Hearsay

Defined supra.

The labels about which Phil is testifying were on the original labeled containers received at Phil's Pharmacy from the supplier at a location outside the present proceeding. For purposes of the current trial, they are considered an out-of-court statement.

The testimony is being introduced to prove that the bottles labeled DLD contained a derivative of opium. Such testimony is offered to prove the truth of the statutory offense asserted in the larceny of a dangerous drug indictment.

Thus, the testimony is inadmissible hearsay.

Exception - Federal Rule Catchall

Where the circumstances are trustworthy, and the evidence of a material fact has high probative value that serves justice, the evidence will be held admissible after notice to the opponent.

As previously discussed, Phil was familiar with the bottles that were taken. Since he has knowledge of the items about which he is testifying, his testimony would be impliedly trustworthy.

Phil's testimony indicated that the drug taken was DLD. The identification of the drug was an integral element of the alleged crime making it a material fact to the charge of larceny of a dangerous drug. Identification of the contents of the stolen bottles had high probative value as to whether the contents were dangerous drugs. Since the bottles and labels were lost, Phil's testimony would be crucial to a finding of guilt or innocence sufficient to serve the interests of justice.

The facts do not indicate whether the prosecution notified Dick's counsel that it intended to introduce Phil's testimony. Assuming it did, the evidence is admissible.

Phil's testimony is admissible under the federal rule catchall exception.

(c) PROSECUTION'S REQUEST - JUDICIAL NOTICE THAT DLD IS A DERIVATIVE OF OPIUM

Logical Relevancy

Defined supra.

The finding as to whether DLD is a derivative of opium has a tendency in reason to prove that it is a dangerous drug falling within the purview of the statute under which Dick is being prosecuted. This statute does not specifically list DLD as a dangerous drug, but does define dangerous drugs to include any derivative of opium. This finding is a disputed fact of consequence to the determination of the State's action against the defendant under the statute.

The prosecution's request is logically relevant.

Judicial Notice (Permissive)

A court may accept facts that are not reasonably subject to dispute and are capable of immediate and accurate determination without the necessity of formal proof.

The prosecution requested the court to take judicial notice that DLD is a derivative of opium. In doing so, it has asked the court to accept as true without formal proof that DLD was a derivative of opium on the basis of an inspection of a standard pharmacological dictionary establishing it as such. Although the statute under which Dick is being prosecuted does not list DLD as a dangerous drug, the prosecution is asserting that this matter is not reasonably subject to dispute. Based on the indisputable accuracy of the dictionary establishing the immediate and accurate determination of DLD as an opiate derivative, there is no necessity of formal proof.

However, the matter upon which the prosecution seeks judicial notice involves an essential element of the crime for which Dick is being charged. Whether DLD is an opiate is subject to dispute. Due process requires the prosecution to establish its case without the court's assistance. The prosecution will not be allowed to "fill in" this essential element without independent evidence of formal proof.

Therefore, the prosecution must prove with formal proof that the drugs in question were derivatives of opium as required under the statute.

The court will not take judicial notice of DLD as a derivative of opium.

(d) TESTIMONY OF WIN REGARDING DICK'S USE OF NARCOTICS DURING MARRIAGE

Logical Relevance

Defined supra.

Win testified that during her marriage to Dick, the latter frequently used narcotics but attempted to conceal that fact from her. Win's testimony has a tendency in reason to prove that Dick stole to support his addiction, a disputed fact of consequence to the determination of the action related to larceny of a dangerous drug.

Win's testimony is logically relevant.

Spousal Privilege - Privilege Not to Testify Against Spouse

At common law, either spouse was disqualified to testify against the other in any civil or criminal action in which the other was a party while the marriage exists.

Win was divorced from Dick at the time her testimony was obtained. Since the marriage no longer existed, the privilege does not apply.

The marital privilege to prevent spousal testimony will not apply.

Spousal Privilege - Privilege for Confidential Marital Communications

Confidential communications between spouses made during marriage are privileged even after the marriage has been terminated.

Dick will assert that his frequent use of narcotics and attempts to conceal it during his marriage were matters that were made out of the presence of third parties because he wished to keep it secret. His nonverbal conduct constituted a confidential communication solely between himself and his spouse. The courts are split as to nonverbal conduct intended to be private and confidential.

However, the State will counter that Win's testimony concerned her mere observations of Dick's conduct in relation to his physical and mental drug condition. Many traditional jurisdictions would find that observations of conduct alone are insufficient for a confidential communication.

In those jurisdictions that would recognize Dick's conduct as a nonverbal confidential communication, either spouse may assert the privilege to prevent the admission of the testimony.

Thus, depending upon the jurisdiction, Dick's objection to Win's testimony may be sufficient to prevent Win's testimony.

EVIDENCE QUESTION #4

PAUL v. CABCO

An automobile owned and operated by Paul collided with a taxicab driven by Don and owned by Cabco. Paul and Don were injured. Vicky, a passenger in Paul's automobile, suffered a broken leg. While she was undergoing necessary surgery to repair the fracture, she suffered a cardiac arrest and died. Action was brought in state court by Paul against Cabco for personal injuries. The parties stipulated to the above facts.

At the trial by jury the following occurred:

A. Paul testified: "After the accident, I went over to the cab. Don was hurting real bad, and Don said, 'This wouldn't have happened if I hadn't been in such a hurry to pick up a fare.'"

B. Cabco's counsel asked Paul on cross-examination if he had ever had a traffic accident. Paul answer: "No." Cabco's counsel then introduced a properly authenticated copy of a three-year old unrelated conviction of Paul for vehicular manslaughter, a felony.

C. Vicky's physician, Doc, testified as a witness for Cabco that, while Vicky was being prepared for surgery, he asked her how the accident happened, and she responded: "Don't tell anybody, Doc, but Paul and I were smoking marijuana. I dropped a lighted joint, and Paul had his head down looking for it when we hit the cab."

Assume that in each instance all appropriate objections were made. Were the items of evidence properly admitted? Discuss.

IRAC OUTLINE SHEET

(I)	(R)	(A)	(C)

EXAMPLE OF PROPER IRAC OUTLINE

PAUL (P) v. CABCO (C)

A. (1) P'S TESTIMONY RE D'S "HURTING REAL BAD"

(I)	(R)	(A)	(C)
LOGICAL RELEVANCE	Tendency In Reason To Prove/Disprove Disputed Fact Consequence To Action	After the accident, I went over to the cab D was hurting real bad (liability?)	Logically Relevant
LAY OPINION	Common Law-Prohibited Modern Law-Admissible		Proper Lay Opinion
	Personal Observations/Facts In Dispute	D was hurting real bad	
	No Better Evidence	Supra	

(2) P'S TESTIMONY RE D'S STATEMENT

(I)	(R)	(A)	(C)
LOGICAL RELEVANCE	Tendency In Reason To Prove/Disprove Disputed Fact	D said "This wouldn't have happened if I hadn't been in such a hurry to pick up a fare"	Logically Relevant
	Consequence To Action	An auto owned & operated by P collided with taxicab driven by D/owned by C P v. C for personal injuries	
HEARSAY	Out-Of-Court Statement	After the accident, I went over to the cab/D said...	Arguable
	Offered For Truth Of Matter Asserted	Wouldn't have happened if I hadn't been in such a hurry to pick up a fare (concerning matter of employment?)	
EXCEPTION: VICARIOUS ADMISSION	Admission By 3rd Party	D said...supra/P v. C	Arguable
	Independent Existence Of Agency Proven	Taxicab driven by D/owned by C	
	Facts Relate To Current Matters	This wouldn't have happened if I hadn't been in such a hurry to pick up a fare	
	Statement Made Within Scope Of Agent's Authority/Employment	Hurrying to pick up a fare (D drove cab for C?)	
EXCEPTION-EXCITED UTTERANCE	Exciting Event	After the accident	Valid Exception
	Stimulus/Spontaneous Statement	After the accident, D said...	
	Relates To Cause Of Excitement	Wouldn't have happened if I hadn't been in hurry supra	
	Personal Knowledge	Taxicab driven by D	
PRESENT SENSE IMPRESSION	Statement Contemporaneous With Event While Perceiving It	After the accident	Valid Exception
	Statement Describes Event	Wouldn't have happened if not hurrying supra	

B. C'S CROSS-EXAMINATION RE: PRIOR ACCIDENT

(I)	(R)	(A)	(C)
LOGICAL RELEVANCE	Tendency In Reason To Prove/Disprove Disputed Fact Consequence To Action	C's counsel asked P on cross-x if he had ever had a traffic accident P v C/prior accident (Fault?)	Logically Relevant
CROSS-EXAMINATION-SCOPE	Common Law: Unrestricted Federal Rules: Matters Put In Issue On Direct Including Credibility	C's counsel asked P on cross-x if he ever had a traffic accident/P answered "No"	Arguable
IMPEACHMENT:CHARACTER FOR HONESTY-PAST CONVICTION OF A CRIME	Common Law - Any Felony F.R.-Allows If Felony Conviction Involves Dishonesty/False Statement F.R.-Allows Any Felony Conviction Unless Probative Value Outweighed By Prejudicial Impact CA- Allows Any Conviction Involving Moral Turpitude	P denied prior traffic accidents supra/prior felony conviction re vehicular manslaughter supra Three year/unrelated supra	Split Of Jurisdictions
IMPEACHMENT: PRIOR INCONSISTENT STATEMENT	Witness Statement Inconsistent With Evidence Offered	P denied prior traffic accidents supra Prior felony conviction supra (collateral?)	Arguable
FOUNDATION	Traditional: Witness Must First Be Asked About Statement Federal Rules: Relax Foundation Requirement	C's counsel asked P if he had ever had a traffic accident/P's answer "no" C introduced authenticated copy of 3 year old felony supra	Proper Foundation
LEGAL RELEVANCE	Probative v Prejudicial	P answered "No"/C's counsel then introduced a properly authenticated copy of a 3 year old unrelated conviction of P for vehicular manslaughter, a felony	Legally Irrelevant

C. DOC'S TESTIMONY RE VICKI'S (V) STATEMENTS

(I)	(R)	(A)	(C)
LOGICAL RELEVANCE	Tendency In Reason To Prove/Disprove Disputed Fact	Doc testified that while V being prepared for surgery, he asked her how accident happened	Logically Relevant
	Consequence To Action	She responded "Don't tell anybody but P & I were smoking marijuana/I dropped a lighted joint & P had his head down looking for it when we hit the cab	
HEARSAY	Out-Of-Court Statement	While V being prepared for surgery, she responded...supra	Hearsay
	Offered For Truth Of Matter Asserted	(Causation?)	
EXCEPTION-DECLARATION AGAINST INTEREST	Declarant A Non-Party To Litigation	P v. C lawsuit V a passenger in P's automobile	Valid Exception
	Declarant Unavailable To Testify	V suffered a cardiac arrest/died	
	Personal Knowledge	V a passenger in P's automobile	
	Against Declarant's Interest	V smoking marijuana (penal interest-civil interest?)	
EXCEPTION-DYING DECLARATION	Declarant Unavailable	V suffered cardiac arrest & died	Invalid Exception
	Believes Death Imminent	Being prepared for surgery supra	
	Relates To Cause Of Death	While undergoing necessary surgery to repair the fracture, suffered cardiac arrest and died	
	Personal Knowledge	"Don't tell/smoking marijuana" supra V a passenger in P's car while she & P smoking supra	
EXCEPTION-STATE OF BODY	Physical Condition At Issue	Paul v. Cabco/fractured leg at issue?	Arguable
	Spontaneous Statement To Treating Physician	While V being prepared for surgery	
	Prove Existence Of Condition	Cause of fractured leg/accident	
PHYSICIAN/PATIENT PRIVILEGE	Doctor/Patient Relationship	While being prepared for surgery...supra	Arguable
	Confidential Information	"Doc, don't tell anybody"	
	Relating To Treatment	Disclosed during diagnosis/treatment	
	Holder-Patient	V's dead (estate liability?)	

EXAMPLE OF IRAC EVIDENCE ISSUE

(I) **Exception - Declaration Against Interest**

(R) A statement may be received into evidence if (1) the person who made the statement is not a party to the action, (2) is unavailable to testify, (3) the statement was within the person's personal knowledge at the time, and (4) the statement was made against an important interest of the declarant.

(A) Although Vicky was a passenger in Paul's car at the time of the accident, she is not (1) a named defendant party in the Paul v. Cabco lawsuit. Her cardiac arrest and subsequent death while being prepared for surgery clearly makes her (2) unavailable to testify at trial. Vicky's statement to Doc was based on her own actions and observations while riding as a passenger in Paul's automobile. Thus, she had (3) personal knowledge that Paul was looking for the joint while driving.

Further, Vicky's comments that she was smoking marijuana was an admission that could subject her to criminal liability at the time she made them. While a majority of jurisdictions would not recognize the admission as against her (4) penal interest, the federal rules would permit it as long as corroborating circumstances exist to verify the accuracy of the statement.

Also, her statements could be an admission against her important proprietary/civil interests since it would imply comparative negligence in any lawsuit that her estate might bring on her behalf.

(C) The testimony may be admissible as a declaration against interest.

SUGGESTED MODEL ANSWER

PAUL v. CABCO

A(1) PAUL'S TESTIMONY RE: "DON HURTING REAL BAD"

Logical Relevance

Evidence is logically relevant if it has any tendency in reason to prove or disprove a disputed fact of consequence to the determination of the action.

Paul testified that after the accident, he went over to the cab. "Don was hurting real bad." Such testimony has a tendency in reason to prove that Don was injured in an auto collision, a disputed fact of consequence to the determination of the action concerning liability.

Paul's testimony is logically relevant.

Lay Opinion

Common law prohibited lay opinion. Modernly, lay opinion will be admissible when it is a result of that witnesses personal observation of facts in dispute and when no better evidence can be reasonably obtained.

Paul's testimony that Don was "hurting real bad" was based on Paul's personal observation of Don in his cab immediately after the traffic accident. Under common law, her testimony was prohibited.

Modernly, the appearance of persons injured at an automobile accident is something about which normal persons regularly form opinions. Since Paul could see Don's appearance, he would be allowed to give an opinion describing Don's apparent physical condition. Such information is rationally based on Paul's personal observation of Don's pain. It would be helpful to the trier of fact in its determination of Don's subsequent statement, a fact in dispute. No better evidence appears to be reasonably obtained to dispute his observations.

Paul's testimony is proper lay opinion.

A(2) PAUL'S TESTIMONY RE: DON'S STATEMENT

Logical Relevance

Defined supra.

Paul testified that Don said "This wouldn't have happened if I hadn't been in such a hurry to pick up a fare." Such testimony has a tendency in reason to prove that Don was negligently driving a cab owned by Cabco, a disputed fact of consequence to the determination of Cabco's liability to Paul for the actions of its employee while on duty.

Paul's testimony is logically relevant.

Hearsay

Hearsay is an out-of-court statement offered to prove the truth of the matter asserted.

Don made the above statement to Paul at the scene of the accident, outside the present proceeding. As such, it is considered an out-of-court statement. Don admitted that the accident would not have occurred if he hadn't been in such a hurry to pick up a fare. Thus, Paul's testimony is being offered to prove a matter of employment and fault, the truth of the matter asserted.

Paul's testimony is inadmissible hearsay.

Exception - Vicarious Admission

Admissions made by a third party may be imputed to another party and may be admissible against that party if independent existence of the agency is proven, the facts relate to current matters, and the statement was made within the scope of the agent's authority or employment.

The taxicab involved in the accident was owned by Cabco but driven by Don. Don is not a defendant in the Paul v. Cabco lawsuit making him a third party to that action. Paul must prove that the cab was owned by Cabco and that Don was Cabco's employee. Independent evidence such as paychecks, W-2's, etc. will suffice. Don's assertion that the accident wouldn't have happened if he hadn't been in such a hurry involves facts related to the cause of the current accident.

Under common law, vicarious admissions were limited to those relating to the nature of the employment. Since the cause of the accident was not directly related to Don's contract to drive a cab, Don was not authorized to speak on behalf of Cabco. His admission would not be chargeable against Cabco.

However, under the federal rules, Don's hurrying to pick up a fare was a matter within the scope of his employment as a taxicab driver. It was made after the accident and during the existence of his employment.

Therefore, vicarious admission is a valid exception.

Exception - Excited Utterance

The statement of any person made at the time of some exciting event and under the stimulus of his excitement may be admissible if it is spontaneous, relates to the cause of the excitement, and is within the personal knowledge of that person.

Don made the statement just after he and Paul collided at which time Don was under the stimulus of this shocking and exciting event. Don's statement was made immediately after the accident when Paul approached Don's cab. Since Don was "hurting real bad" from the injuries he sustained, he appeared to have had no time to calculate or deliberate a misstatement. Therefore, his statement was spontaneous.

Don's description of his own hurrying related to the cause of the accident. Since it was he who was hurrying to pick up a fare, he had personal knowledge of his own driving.

Excited utterance is a valid exception.

Exception - Present Sense Impression

The federal rules permit admission of a statement made by a person contemporaneous with the event while perceiving it and which describes or explains that event or condition.

Don's statement was made so soon after the accident that it was contemporaneous with the event while he was acting within the time that he was hurting and perceiving himself as injured at the scene. Don was describing his hurrying as the cause of the event.

Present sense impression is a valid exception.

B. CABCO'S CROSS-EXAMINATION RE: PAUL'S PRIOR ACCIDENT/ FELONY CONVICTION

Logical Relevance

Defined supra.

Cabco's counsel asked Paul on cross-examination if he'd ever had a traffic accident. Such a question has a tendency in reason to prove Paul's prior driving record, a disputed fact of consequence to the determination of fault in this present action.

Cabco's question is logically relevant.

Cross-Examination - Scope

Common law permits unrestricted cross-examination. However, the federal rules restrict cross-examination to any matter related to a subject raised on direct examination including the witness' credibility.

There are no facts to indicate that Paul's own driving record was put into issue during direct examination. Under common law, such unrestricted cross-examination would still be permitted. Under the federal rules, if the intent of Cabco's counsel was to demonstrate Paul's lack of truthfulness by his denial of prior traffic accidents despite a later showing of a prior felony conviction for vehicular manslaughter, such cross-examination may be used to demonstrate Paul's lack of credibility.

The court may use its discretion when permitting inquiry into additional matters and when deciding whether Cabco's counsel exceeded its scope of cross-examination.

Impeachment of Character for Honesty - Past Conviction of a Crime

Common law permits impeachment by any felony, whether pertinent to truthfulness or veracity or not. The federal rules allow impeachment based on a prior felony conviction if that conviction involves dishonesty or a false statement. If the prior conviction is any other felony, the court must weigh the probative value of the evidence against the undue prejudice to the witness. California allows impeachment evidence of any felony conviction involving moral turpitude.

Paul denied prior traffic accidents. However, Paul's felony record showed an unrelated vehicular manslaughter conviction three years earlier. Under common law, the felony conviction is admissible for impeachment. Even though a prior conviction within ten years is considered impeachable evidence, there are no facts to suggest that this crime involved a showing of dishonesty or a false statement. Therefore, under the federal rules, the court will weigh the probative value of the evidence against the unfair prejudice to Paul. Since Paul is now suing for personal injuries arising out a current automobile accident, it would appear that introduction of this three year old, unrelated felony, would have minimal probative value and would result in undue prejudice to Paul's case. Further, the felony does not involve moral turpitude. Thus, it would not constitute proper impeachment evidence in California.

Cabco's cross-examination was proper impeachment of character for honesty in common law jurisdictions. It is arguable whether it is admissible under the federal rules.

Impeachment - Prior Inconsistent Statement

A witness' credibility may be attacked by a showing that the witness engaged in prior inconsistent acts regarding the matters to which he or she has given testimony.

Paul had a prior felony vehicular manslaughter conviction which he denied on cross-examination. The showing of this conviction was inconsistent with his denial. However, this conviction was unrelated to the accident currently being tried. It did not concern the parties, events or time of the accident which are the subject matter of this lawsuit. As a collateral matter, the evidence is inadmissible.

However, if the court rules in its discretion that it is admissible for purposes of impeachment, Cabco's counsel must show that a proper foundation was laid.

Laying a Foundation

Traditional jurisdictions require that a witness be asked about a statement before it can be introduced. The federal rules have relaxed foundational requirements.

Cabco's counsel asked Paul whether he'd ever had a traffic accident. Paul answered "No". Paul was given an opportunity to admit or explain it before Cabco's counsel introduced the properly authenticated copy of Paul's prior conviction. In both jurisdictions, a proper foundation was laid.

Legal Relevance

No evidence may be admitted where its probative value is substantially outweighed by its prejudicial impact.

Paul will assert that his answer of "No" to Cabco's question previously discussed followed by the introduction of an unrelated, three year old vehicular manslaughter conviction would only confuse the jury. It could lead them to believe that if Paul had a past history of illegal driving, he may have engaged in unsafe driving on this occasion. Such inference could prejudice their minds as to liability for the accident. The prejudicial impact of such evidence substantially outweighs its probative value.

The evidence should be excluded as legally irrelevant.

C. DOC'S TESTIMONY RE: VICKY'S STATEMENT

Logical Relevance

Defined supra.

Doc testified that while Vicky was being prepared for surgery, he asked her how the accident occurred. She responded that Paul was looking for a marijuana joint she'd dropped when the accident occurred. Such a statement has a tendency in reason to prove that Paul's own negligence was the cause of the accident, a disputed fact of consequence to the determination of the action.

Doc's testimony is logically relevant.

Hearsay

Defined supra.

Since Vicky made her statement while she was at the hospital being prepared for surgery, it was an out-of-court statement. Cabco's counsel is using Vicky's statement to prove that Paul's act of looking for the dropped marijuana joint while driving impeded his ability to properly operate his vehicle and was the cause of his collision with Don, the truth of the matter asserted.

Doc's testimony is inadmissible hearsay.

Exception - Declaration Against Interest

A statement may be received into evidence if the person who made the statement is not a party to the action, is unavailable to testify, the statement was within the person's personal knowledge at the time, and the statement was made against an important interest of the declarant.

Although Vicky was a passenger in Paul's car at the time of the accident, she is not a named defendant party in the Paul v. Cabco lawsuit. Her cardiac arrest and subsequent death while being prepared for surgery clearly makes her unavailable to testify at trial. Vicky's statement to Doc was based on her own actions and observations while riding as a passenger in Paul's automobile. Thus, she had personal knowledge that Paul was looking for the joint while driving.

Further, Vicky's comments that she was smoking marijuana was an admission that could subject her to criminal liability at the time she made them. While a majority of jurisdictions would not recognize the admission as against her penal interest, the federal rules would permit it as long as corroborating circumstances exist to verify the accuracy of the statement.

Also, her statements could be an admission against her important proprietary/civil interests since it would imply comparative negligence in any lawsuit that her estate might bring on her behalf.

The testimony may be admissible as a declaration against interest.

Exception - Dying Declaration

Statements of a victim regarding the cause or circumstances of his impending death are admissible if the declarant is unavailable, believed the death was imminent when making the statement, the statement relates to the cause of death, and is within the declarant's personal knowledge.

Vicky suffered a cardiac arrest. Her subsequent death clearly makes her unavailable to testify. She made the statement while being prepared for surgery to repair a fractured leg. There was no indication at that moment Vicky was fearful of death or believed that such surgery would result in imminent death. Further, her statement related to the marijuana joint that was dropped in Paul's car. It was unrelated to the cardiac arrest that was the ultimate cause of her death. Although Vicky had personal knowledge of the joint being smoked in Paul's car, this would not be sufficient to satisfy the other elements.

Dying declaration is an invalid exception.

Exception - State of Body

Where a person's physical condition at a specified time is in issue, that person's spontaneous statements made to a treating physician are admissible to prove the existence of the condition.

Since Vicky was not a party to the Paul v. Cabco lawsuit, it appears that her physical condition was not actually at issue.

However, she <u>made</u> the statement while being prepared for <u>surgery</u> and in response to Doc's question about how the accident occurred. Under such circumstances, it appears that her statement was <u>spontaneous</u>.

Further, Vicky's statement to "Doc," her <u>treating</u> <u>physician</u> that she had been smoking marijuana was vital information for her doctor for purposes of diagnosing, <u>treating</u> and selecting anesthetic or considering alternative means of repairing her fractured leg.

Depending upon whether Vicky's physical condition is at issue, so will determine whether state of body will act as a valid exception.

<u>Physician-Patient Privilege</u>

A patient has a <u>privilege</u> to <u>refuse</u> to disclose, and to <u>prevent</u> his <u>physician</u> from <u>disclosing</u>, any information relating to <u>treatment</u> obtained by the physician while treating the patient.

Paul will argue that Vicky made her statement to Doc while being prepared for surgery and in response to his inquiry as to how the accident occurred. She specifically told Doc "Don't tell anybody." Therefore, the <u>information</u> was a <u>confidential</u> communication arising from a <u>physician/patient</u> <u>relationship</u> and disclosed during the course of Vicky's diagnosis and treatment. However, her statement arguably does <u>not</u> <u>relate</u> to <u>treatment</u> as it was gratuitously offered as an explanation as to the cause of the accident. It would have no bearing on her actual treatment.

Even though Vicky died, the <u>privilege</u> <u>belongs</u> to the <u>patient</u>, and it may be asserted by her personal estate representative. However, if they do not, the privilege will be extinguished and Doc may be compelled to testify.

EVIDENCE QUESTION #5

STATE v. DAN/ELLEN

Dan and Ellen, husband and wife, were tried jointly for shoplifting but were represented by different attorneys. The prosecution contended that the defendants entered Store, that while Ellen distracted the clerk, Dan put a pocket calculator valued at $100.00 in his pocket, and that the defendants then left with the calculator. At the trial the following events occurred:

(a) The prosecution called as a witness the manager of Store and asked him whether the missing calculator could possibly have been sold at any time prior to the time Dan and Ellen entered Store. The manager said, "No, I have carefully checked the sales records which we keep in the ordinary course of our business; in those records our clerks enter a description of every item valued at more than $25.00 immediately after it is sold. The records show no earlier sales of that type calculator."

(b) The prosecution called as a witness Store's clerk, who testified that as the defendants left Store, he noticed that the calculator was missing from a display stand; that he ran to the door and shouted loudly, "Hey, come back!"; and that the defendants ran to an intersection where they boarded a public bus.

(c) The prosecution called as a witness Wat, who testified that one week before the event charged in the information, Dan and Ellen entered his store and that, while Ellen was asking Wat questions about some merchandise, he saw Dan place a tape recorder in his overcoat pocket.

(d) At the close of the prosecution's case in chief, over Dan's objection, Ellen's attorney called Ellen as a witness.

Assume all appropriate objections were timely made. How should the court have ruled on the admissibility of the evidence offered in items (a), (b), (c) and how should the court have ruled on Dan's objection in item (d)? Discuss.

IRAC OUTLINE SHEET

(I)	(R)	(A)	(C)

EXAMPLE OF PROPER IRAC OUTLINE

STATE v. DAN (D) AND ELLEN (E) FOR SHOPLIFTING

(a) MANAGER'S (M) TESTIMONY RE: STORE RECORDS

(I)	(R)	(A)	(C)
LOGICAL RELEVANCY	Tendency In Reason To Prove/Disprove Disputed Fact	M called as a witness of store M asked whether missing calculator sold at any time prior to time D/E entered store	Logically Relevant
	Consequence To Action	Record shows no earlier sales of that type calculator (stolen?)	
BEST EVIDENCE RULE	Content Of A Writing	"I have carefully checked sales record" Records show no earlier sales	Arguable
	Original Must Be Produced Unless Unavailable Exception-Voluminous Writing	Sales record available?	
HEARSAY	Out-Of-Court Statement	Sales records kept in ordinary course of our business	Hearsay
	Offered For Truth Of Matter Asserted	Clerks enter description of every item valued > $25 immediately after sold Records show no earlier sales of that type calculator (stolen?)	
EXCEPTION- BUSINESS RECORD	Kept Within Regular Course Of Business	M said sales records kept in ordinary course of business	Valid Exception
	Entrant Has Personal Knowledge	In that record clerks enter a description of item valued at more than $25	
	Business Duty To Report	Description entered immediately after item sold	
	Entry Made At/Near Time Of Event Trustworthy	Entry made immediately after sale Records kept ordinary course of business	

(b) CLERK'S TESTIMONY RE: DEFENDANT'S FLIGHT

(I)	(R)	(A)	(C)
LOGICAL RELEVANCY	Tendency In Reason To Prove/Disprove Disputed Fact	He ran to door & shouted loudly,"Hey, come back" D/E ran to intersection where they boarded a public bus	Logically Relevant
	Consequence To Action	(consciousness of guilt from shoplifting?)	
HEARSAY	Out-Of-Court Statement	Yelled/defendants ran/boarded public bus	Arguable
	Offered For Truth Of Matter Asserted	Shoplifting	
EXCLUSION:EFFECT UPON A LISTENER	Words Offered To Show Effect Upon Listener	"Hey, come back" Defendants ran/boarded public bus supra (conduct of guilt?) (did defendants hear?)	Invalid Exclusion
EXCLUSION NON-ASSERTIVE CONDUCT (Nonhearsay)	Conduct Not Intended As Substitute For Words	Clerk shouted "Hey, come back" Defendants ran to bus (conduct substitute for words of guilt?)	Fed/Cal Nonhearsay Morgan Jurisdictions Hearsay
EXCEPTION-ADMISSION BY CONDUCT	Party To The Litigation	D and E defendants	
	Conduct Asserts Belief Inconsistent With Position At Trial	Clerk shouted "Hey, come back" D/E ran/boarded bus supra (consciousness guilt through conduct?) Pled not guilty for shoplifting	Valid Exception

(c) WAT'S (W) TESTIMONY RE: DAN'S PRIOR SHOPLIFTING

(I)	(R)	(A)	(C)
LOGICAL RELEVANCY	Tendency In Reason To Prove/Disprove Disputed Fact	W testified that one week before the event charged in the information, D & E entered W's store/while E asked questions about merchandise, he saw D place tape recorder in overcoat pocket	Logically Relevant
	Consequence To Action	(propensity to shoplift?)	

(I)	(R)	(A)	(C)
CHARACTER EVIDENCE	Bad Character To Prove Propensity	Prosecutor called W/testified E asked questions/D placed tape recorder in pocket supra (proof of actions in conformity to present store theft?)	Improper Character
	Defendant Must Open The Door	No facts	
LIMITED ADMISSIBILITY	Evidence Inadmissible For One Purpose May Be Admissible For Another	E asked questions/D stole merchandise	Limited Admissibility
LEGAL RELEVANCE	Probative v. Prejudicial	Modus operandi (would jury convict based on similarity?)	Arguable

(d) EARL'S (E) TESTIMONY

(I)	(R)	(A)	(C)
LOGICAL RELEVANCY	Tendency In Reason To Prove/Disprove Disputed Fact	E called as a witness	Logically Relevant
	Consequence To Action	(will testimony show guilt?)	
SPOUSAL TESTIMONIAL PRIVILEGE	Marital Relationship	D/E husband and wife	Valid Privilege
	Privilege Not To Testify	Over D's objection E called to testify	
HOLDER OF PRIVILEGE	Majority: Party Spouse	D	Arguable
	Federal: Witness Spouse	E (voluntary testimony?)	
	California: Witness Spouse	(balance E s right to fair trial v D's right to privilege)	
	Minority: Witness Spouse		

EXAMPLE OF IRAC EVIDENCE ISSUE

(I) **Limited Admissibility**

(R) Evidence that is (1) inadmissible for one purpose is not necessarily inadmissible for another purpose and may be (2) offered for other purposes rather than to show probable conduct.

(A) The State will contend that it is seeking to (1) admit the evidence of similar circumstances of theft, not to show Dan and Ellen's probable conduct, but (2) rather to show their modus operandi as to the circumstances of the theft.

In both instances, Ellen distracted the sales clerk by asking questions while Dan stole the merchandise. Such conduct indicates a common plan or scheme.

It appears that the evidence would be admitted for the limited purpose of showing the modus operandi of the defendants.

(C) It will be incumbent upon the court to give the jury a limiting instruction as to the purpose for which they may consider Wat's testimony.

SUGGESTED MODEL ANSWER

STATE v. DAN AND ELLEN

(a) MANAGER'S TESTIMONY RE: STORE RECORDS

Logical Relevance

Evidence is logically relevant if it has any tendency in reason to prove or disprove a disputed fact of consequence to the determination of the action.

The prosecution called store manager as a witness. He was asked whether the missing calculator could have been sold at any time prior to the time Dan and Ellen entered the store. Manager answered that the records showed no earlier sales of that type of calculator. His testimony has a tendency in reason to prove that the calculator in question was stolen by Dan and Ellen rather than sold to them, the disputed fact of consequence to the determination of the shoplifting action.

Therefore, Manager's testimony is logically relevant.

Best Evidence Rule

In order to prove the contents of a writing, the original must be produced unless it is unavailable.

Manager testified that he "carefully checked the sales records" which showed no earlier sales of a $100 calculator such as the one Dan and Ellen are charged with shoplifting. Manager is, therefore, testifying as to the contents of the written sales records. There are no facts to indicate that the original sales records were unavailable and could not have been produced at trial.

However, if the records were so voluminous that it would be impractical to produce them, under the voluminous writing exception, the original writing need not be produced.

Here, the facts are unclear as to the bulk of the sales records. Thus, Manager's testimony would be admissible only if the court finds the exception to the best evidence rule has been satisfied.

Hearsay

Hearsay is an out-of-court statement offered to prove the truth of the matter asserted.

Manager is testifying as to the documentation contained in the sales records. Since the records were prepared and kept at the store, outside the present proceeding, they constitute an out-of-court statement.

Manager testified that the clerk enters a description of the sale of every item valued at more than $25.00 immediately after the sale. The State is offering this evidence to prove that the clerk was required to document every item sold over $25.00, but the record showed no earlier sale of that type of $100.00 calculator. The lack of entry proves that it was not sold but stolen by Dan and Ellen, the truth of the matter asserted.

The testimony is inadmissible hearsay.

Exception - Business Record

Business records kept within the regular course of business activity may be admitted if the entrant has personal knowledge, had a business duty to report, the entry was made at or near the time of the event, and the records are trustworthy.

The Manager stipulated that the sales records are kept in the ordinary course of the Store's business. In that record, the clerk responsible for making the sale enters a description of every item valued at more than $25.00, ensuring the entrant's personal knowledge of any sale over that amount.

Further, the clerks were required to enter a description of the sale immediately after the item was sold. Thus, the clerks had a business duty to report the sale in the written sales record if it had been made.

Since the clerks made record entries immediately after a sale over $25.00, the entry, if the sale had been made, would have been at or near the time of the sale event. There are no facts to indicate that the record was not trustworthy.

Manager's testimony will be admissible under the business record exception.

(b) CLERK'S TESTIMONY RE: DEFENDANT'S FLIGHT FROM STORE

Logical Relevance

Defined supra.

The clerk testified that he ran to the door and shouted loudly to Dan and Ellen, "Hey, come back". This statement, coupled with Dan and Ellen's act of running to the intersection where they boarded the public bus, has a tendency in reason to prove their consciousness of guilt, a disputed fact of consequence to the determination of the shoplifting action.

The clerk's testimony is logically relevant.

Hearsay

Defined supra.

The clerk testified that after he yelled, Dan and Ellen ran and boarded a bus, conduct deemed an out-of-court statement as to their guilt. Further, the State offered the testimony to prove that Dan and Ellen shoplifted and then ran, the truth of the matter asserted.
Therefore, the evidence is inadmissible hearsay.

Exclusion - Effect Upon the Listener

Words offered to show their effect upon the listener, not the truth of the matter asserted, will act as a hearsay exclusion.

The State is offering the clerk's words, "Hey, come back", to show that the effect of hearing these words caused Dan and Ellen to run from the store to avoid capture for shoplifting the calculator.

However, even though the clerk testified that he shouted loudly, there is no evidence that Dan and Ellen actually heard the words. They may have been running to catch the bus because it was leaving, not because they thought they would be caught for shoplifting.

Therefore, this exclusion is invalid. The testimony is inadmissible.

Exclusion - Nonassertive Conduct

In the federal and California jurisdictions, conduct not intended as a substitute for words is non-hearsay.

After the clerk shouted loudly, "Hey, come back", Dan and Ellen ran to board a bus. The State will assert that it is unlikely Dan and Ellen intended their conduct to substitute for words related to their guilt. If so, their conduct is non-hearsay.

It appears that in the federal and California jurisdictions, the conduct of the defendants would be admitted as non-hearsay.

However, jurisdictions which follow the Morgan view consider all conduct, assertive and non-assertive, to be hearsay. In such jurisdictions, the State could only admit the evidence upon the showing of an applicable exception to the hearsay rule.

Exception - Admission by Conduct

Where a party to the litigation, through conduct, asserts a belief inconsistent with a position taken at trial, such conduct is an exception to the hearsay rule.

Dan and Ellen are party defendants in the shoplifting trial. As previously discussed, Dan and Ellen's conduct of running to board a bus after the clerk shouted, "Hey, come back", arguably exhibits conduct demonstrating their consciousness of guilt.

Further, this conduct infers their belief of guilt which is inconsistent with their plea of not guilty at the current shoplifting trial.

The evidence is admissible as an admission by conduct.

(c) WAT'S TESTIMONY RE: DAN'S PRIOR SHOPLIFTING

Logical Relevance

Defined supra.

Wat testified that one week before the event charged in the information, Dan and Ellen entered Wat's store. While Ellen asked him questions about merchandise, he saw Dan place a tape recorder in his overcoat pocket. Wat's testimony has a tendency in reason to prove that Dan and Ellen had the propensity to shoplift in the same manner in the present case. Their modus operandi is the disputed fact of consequence to the determination of the current shoplifting action.

Thus, Wat's testimony is logically relevant.

Character Evidence

The prosecution may not introduce evidence of the defendants' bad character to prove his propensity to commit the crime charged unless the defendant has first opened the door to his own character.

The prosecution called Wat who testified that while Ellen asked questions, Dan stole from his store. Such testimony was intended to establish their bad character to act in the same manner in the present shoplifting action.

However, since the defendants have not yet first opened the door by introducing any evidence of their good character, the prosecution may not introduce evidence of their bad character in Wat's store to show a propensity to commit the crime charged.

This testimony is improper character evidence.

Limited Admissibility

Evidence that is inadmissible for one purpose is not necessarily inadmissible for another purpose and may be offered for purposes other than to show probable conduct.

The State will contend that it is seeking to admit the evidence of similar circumstances of theft, not to show Dan and Ellen's probable conduct, but rather to show their modus operandi as to the circumstances of the theft.

In both instances, Ellen distracted the sales clerk by asking questions while Dan stole the merchandise. Such conduct indicates a common plan or scheme.

It appears that the evidence would be admitted for the limited purpose of showing the modus operandi of the defendants.

It will be incumbent upon the court to give the jury a limiting instruction as to the purpose for which they may consider Wat's testimony.

Legal Relevance

No evidence may be admitted where its probative value is substantially outweighed by its prejudicial impact.

Dan and Ellen will argue that Wat's testimony concerning similar thefts of the exact type for which they are currently charged would lead the jury to believe that if they had once been seen shoplifting in a similar fashion, they must be guilty in the present case. Thus, the jury is certain to convict them if such evidence is admitted.

The State will rebut that both of the crimes were committed in exactly the same manner. Both Wat and the clerk are able to specifically identify Dan and Ellen as the perpetrators. Therefore, the testimony has probative value.

On balance, it would appear that the probative effect of the evidence against Dan and Ellen is not outweighed by its prejudicial impact.

Wat's testimony should be admitted.

(d) ELLEN'S TESTIMONY

Logical Relevance

Defined supra.

Ellen was called as a witness. Her testimony has a tendency in reason to prove information vital to her shoplifting defense, a disputed fact of consequence to the determination of the criminal action.

The evidence is logically relevant.

Spousal Privilege - Privilege Not To Testify Against Spouse

At common law, either spouse was disqualified to testify against the other in any civil or criminal action in which the other was a party while the marriage exists.

Dan and Ellen are husband and wife. As such, the necessary marital relationship exists between them. Dan has objected to Ellen's testimony in an effort to protect his privilege by preventing Ellen from testifying.

Thus, the privilege exists.

Holder of the Privilege

The holder of the privilege is the party entitled to invoke the privilege.

In the majority of jurisdictions, the party spouse is the holder of the privilege. In such a case, Dan, as the non-testifying spouse, would be the holder of the privilege and is entitled to prevent Ellen from testifying.

In the federal, minority and California jurisdictions, the witness spouse is the holder of the privilege. In such jurisdictions, Ellen would be the holder of the privilege. Since Ellen's own attorney called her to testify, she appears to be doing so voluntarily. Dan could do nothing to prevent her testimony.

In the case of a conflict, the court will balance the Sixth Amendment right to a fair trial against the marital privilege.

Ellen would argue that her right to a fair trial includes the right to give testimony on her own behalf. It is likely that the court would consider the right to defend against criminal liability to outweigh the marital privilege, even if by so testifying, the other spouse is implicated in the crime.

Dan's right to prevent Ellen's testimony will depend upon the law in the jurisdiction where the case is being tried.